Thinking
with
EXCELLENCE

Paul R. Shockley, Ph.D.
& Raul F. Prezas, Ph.D.

Thinking
with
EXCELLENCE

Navigating the College Journey & Beyond

Foreword by James E. Towns. Ph.D.

This work is dedicated to students past, present,
and future who are willing to be so daring to think with excellence;
you are the heroes we need for a brighter tomorrow!

ACKNOWLEDGEMENTS

This collaboration between two scholars from two different colleges at a public university, namely, a philosopher and a speech-language pathologist, arose out of shared awareness, concern, and comparable conversations with students. Many students don't know how to best prepare for and navigate through the vast waters of the college and university experience. Burdened with the knowledge that every student receives a transformative education that will best prepare them for this ever-changing world, we have put together a wide array of "navigational" resources and tools to ease the transition as they begin to untie themselves from their moorings and enter into what could become one of their greatest adventures!

We are not only indebted to the Center for Teaching and Learning for their efforts to equip faculty at Stephen F. Austin State University (SFA), but also to our colleagues and administrators who encouraged inter-professional collaboration. Special thanks to Dr. Joyce Johnston (Chair) and the Division of Multidisciplinary Programs, Dr. Robbie Steward (Chair) and the Department of Human Services, Dr. James E. Towns, Regent Professor within the Department of Language, Culture, and Communication, and Dr. Steve H. Bullard, Provost/Vice President for Academic Affairs at SFA.

We are also deeply appreciative to Dr. Raul R. Prezas and Dr. Sylvia M. Prezas, both seasoned educators, for their counsel. Moreover, we are grateful to all those who contributed to the development and success of this work, including the students (especially Kay Mesecher who assisted with editing) who inspire us each and every day!

Lastly, we could not complete this project if it were not for the support, grace, and understanding of our families. Thank you! Each of you are so dearly loved!

CONTENTS

LIFE-SAVING TIPS

The following are common questions asked or weighty problems shared by students in an informal setting:

TOPIC LIST

Anchor Yourself in Learning! Critical Terms to Know

If you are unfamiliar with these terms, then it is important to review them prior to reading the book.

What is the Major Difference between a College and a University?

What is A Priori vs. A Posteriori?

What is Convocation?

What is Credit and Debt? Should I Open a Credit Card?

What's a GPA?

What are Loans?

What is Plagiarism?

What is Rationalism vs. Empiricism?

What does STEM mean?

What is a Study or Travel Abroad?

What is a Syllabus?

What is Work-Study?

FOREWORD BY DR. JAMES E. TOWNS

Regents Professor, Distinguished Professor
Stephen F. Austin State University

The Paradigm of Excellence

"Excellence is an art won by training and habituation:
we do not act rightly because we have virtue or excellence,
but we rather have these because we have acted rightly...
we are what we repeatedly do. Excellence, then,
is not an act, but a habit."[1]

—WILL DURANT, *THE STORY OF PHILOSOPHY*

When considering the poignancy of professors writing accomplishments, I proceed from my own philosophy of teaching. This educational mantra stipulates that a university is a market place of ideas, education is the fusion of learning and living, and instruction enhances the ability to resolve life issues. My teaching paradigm has strengthened my belief that perception is the key to communication. As a professor that has more than five decades of teaching, I would make this book required reading for every student and educator. The following shows how this book entitled, *Thinking with Excellence: Navigating the College Journey and Beyond* can absolutely transform your educational experience.

The foundations of perception may be understood in the following:

My paradigm/value/belief system forms the way I perceive.

My perception forms the way I think.

---

[1]   Will Durant, *The Story of Philosophy* (New York: Pocket Books, 1926, 2006), 98.

Intelligent thinking is innate yet can be enhanced through these educational principles and hopefully leads to a fulfilling life and career in which every day is a learning experience for every student especially first-generation college students. Nourishment for the mind includes reading and studying. Life is best mastered when prioritized, which is exercising the mind. It takes less time to produce results from the higher priority of activities. Exercising the mind is as important as exercising the body in order to keep healthy and focused. Sometimes the best way to combat the threat of stress is to step away from the situation and rest or meditate. It regulates and increases the body's ability to handle stimuli from any situation.

The thoughts/reasoning/decisions form the way I feel.

My thoughts form the way I feel

My feelings form the way I behave/act.

Emotions can be amazing as well as frightening. They are a huge part of stress. There is evidence that chronic emotional stress can be associated with disease. People who have good emotional health have ways to deal with stress.

Nourishment for the emotions is making sure that your reactions to situation are normal. To avoid emotional problems as much as possible, it is important to understand the process you go through to get to a certain emotion. Recognize your emotion and why you are having that emotion. People under stress can be emotional, depressed, anxious and irritable.

Exercising your emotions is easier when you can identify the process they take to get into your being. In the emotions case exercising is controlling your emotions. When stress enters the body for long periods of time the body begins to wear out and your emotions start to unravel. Rest is a method to curb stress and not let it enter your emotions. This form of emotional rest is sometimes called quieting of the mind. The point to quiet time is to listen to what your emotions are telling you. If you create a positive awareness of your feelings, then your behavior will change and you will be able to handle situations and stressors.

My behavior forms my character.

My character forms my destiny!

Dr. Paul R. Shockley and Dr. Raul F. Prezas have enhanced the educational experiences of first-generation students. I refer to these educators as my young reverse mentors. Mentoring is usually the senior mentoring the junior. In my case these two junior professionals are mentoring me in many areas of teaching. What a serendipitous experience in one's profession!

Nacogdoches, Texas

PREFACE

A Transformational Journey

"We build too many walls and not enough bridges."

—Sir Isaac Newton

Thinking with Excellence is for first-generation students in mind, namely, those who are the first in their families to seek a formal education. Broad enough for those attending high school, secondary education, or graduate studies, and easy to grasp, *Thinking with Excellence* will give students a pathway, a mindset, and a skillset to help maximize their educational experience and potential no matter their season in life, historical context, or situational setting. *Thinking with Excellence* will also help those who have educational experience but need a reminder of the basics, a recalibration of sorts. Moreover, this practical guide will also aid the educator to help reach students where they are in an effort to take them on the journey where they need to go. Education is pleasurable and we are privileged to offer this brief synopsis, a primer, of hard and worthwhile lessons learned to those who seek to flourish educationally in the most dynamic ways. What you will discover is that you will not only have an incredible starting point, or springboard, for a transformational educational experience, but you will also have the means to apply these tools of wisdom to all areas of daily living. A rich, textured life is possible! *Think with Excellence!*

The chapters in this book address specific areas with topics ranging from how to succeed in the classroom to how to be happy with the decisions you make in life. Each chapter culminates with a section on "Lifesaving Tips."

These sections offer additional guidance related to common questions and concerns that have been shared by students and professionals. Most of the questions posed and responses provided come out of informal conversations. At the end of the book, there is a supplemental section dedicated to "anchor" terms that are critical for college students. While it is not an exhaustive list, the anchor terms provide a foundation for understanding the college/university environment and beyond.

"Home is behind, the world ahead,
And there are many paths to tread
Through shadows to the edge of night,
Until the stars are all alight.
Then world behind and home ahead,
We'll wander back and home to bed.
Mist and twilight, cloud and shade,
Away shall fade! Away shall fade!"

—J. R. R. Tolkien, *The Fellowship of the Ring*

INTRODUCTION

First Day

"The nectar is in the Journey."

—John J. McDermott

The university comes alive as it transforms from its slumbering summer to receive her students in preparation for the first day. In one morning, the dorms change from empty rooms and desolate hallways to young life bustling with personalities, a stream of colors, and personal belongings; giving a glimpse into what students anticipate, love, and need. A heightened sense of expectation touches their senses. Transitions are experienced as students move from what is familiar towards what is unfamiliar. Thus, it can be a fascinating and even powerful emotional convergence involving feelings of excitement, hopes, and, yes, anxiety. See, for many, security is now replaced with uncertainty, a network of family and friends for strangers, and decisions already made to actually make "free" choices. Ah! The taste of freedom is at hand with all of its joys and burdens, opportunities and privileges, consequences and personal responsibilities. Beliefs will be challenged, perspectives enlarged, and lessons learned; change is in the air.

"It is only with gratitude that life becomes rich."

—Dietrich Bonhoeffer

While enthusiasm exudes from the faces of those moving from home to college and university "habitations," many parents/caregivers and loved ones are seen in the background going over lists, hurrying in and out of the vehicles and residential buildings, making sure all is set for the "adult" they love. Thousands upon thousands of hours, resources, energy, joys and tears, celebrations shared and significant lessons learned, one's loved one is moving from a secure haven into unchartered waters. Underneath the practical details, there is a sharing of excitement but also a specific pain a parent or guardian can only know. Time refuses to slow down for any circumstance. Time is not sympathetic to personal and meaningful losses; time neither knows nor cares. Parents and family members wave to their loved ones and return home to a quiet oddity, a troubling calmness, a certain stillness that leaves many families strangely uncomfortable. For many, they find themselves looking at each other after years of raising their child and think, "Who is the person sitting across from me? I recognize the face, but to be honest, I no longer know the person." A new adventure of re-connecting to one's spouse can occur. Intentionality is required. Excitement, hope, and yes, even anxiety may manifest here as well.

But for students, the faces seen and heard all their lives are replaced with new ones. This transition from what one has always known to what is foreign may not only be difficult, but within oneself, two significant universal longings emerge to the forefront of their minds though perhaps not verbally expressed to each other, namely, the search for security and acceptance. And for many, family dynamics may be different. Some students may be traveling to college by themselves. Perhaps the families of some students are unable to accompany them, for various reasons, or they are not a part of their lives. It is possible, for example, that some students do not have the security and support everyone longs for from their families. Moreover, some students attending college may be doing so later in life and following a non-traditional path. For all students who are attending a college, university, or even technical school, regardless of the time in their lives, means, or circumstances, the emotions, fears, anxiety, and insecurities exist.

We Long for Security

We long for security. Home is what we know. Even though some of us may be moving out from troubling, if not painful, circumstances, we find comfort in the familiar; we know where we are and with whom we are engaging. But walking onto a college or university campus, whether young or old, we are facing something altogether new and perhaps even foreign to our previous experiences. Navigating around college buildings, following new procedures, meeting deadlines, and finding where we should go can be exciting but also very confusing. Seeing hundreds or even thousands of new faces, hearing different voices, taking new classes, exploring new topics, and meeting new teachers is overwhelming for many of us. Even if we like change, the comforts of the customary, what we are used to, generate a certain sense of security; we now suddenly feel like a "fish out of water" as they say. Perhaps more importantly, none of us want to appear anxious, confused, or hurting.

We Long to Belong

We long to belong, to be accepted, to fit in, and to be valued by others. We leave the people we know to unknown faces, new ways, and a wide array of personalities. We go from people asking us questions to no one asking us anything. We move from being valued for our high school accomplishments, reputation, successes, friendships made, and good times shared, to an almost clean slate. Everyone, in essence, is at the same table, on the same "playing field;" we have to start over again. In fact, each level of education (i.e., high school; undergraduate degree; graduate degree) seems to be a rebirth of sorts. Even so, possibilities and opportunities await us and can be experienced!

New Beginnings

The college and university can be a fabulous social "re-start." Some of us never had a charitable, kind, loving, or wholesome childhood. Teenage years can be quite tumultuous physically, emotionally, and spiritually. Problems at home, bullies at school, awkward moments, total misrepresentations, and costly mistakes can now be left behind; a new beginning is possible.

Furthermore, some of us have struggled with understanding who we are, what we are, and who we should be. Some of us wish we were someone else altogether; we don't like who we are or what we have become.

Indeed, college and university life can be a chance to begin anew with a "makeover." While not changing our own uniqueness, we can start making new friends, enhancing our strengths, tasting new freedoms that go beyond the worn out clichés, cliques, and "labeled" statuses unfairly given to us on the social spectrum. It is meaningful to watch how confidence builds as we move from our first year to our semester of graduation; we are coming into our own. Thus, learning from our past and growing from it, we can take who we are and seize the riches of what the college and university life have to offer, going beyond whatever we thought possible. But how?

Think with Excellence

Think with excellence! The most exceptional students we have encountered are not necessarily those with chiseled physiques, fine clothing, hot cars, or a "swag" that makes everyone swoon. No, the students who rise to the top, and those who make a life-giving difference, are the ones who know how to think with excellence. In fact, we contend that many of our challenges in life and in our society are due to two critical problems: (1) inadequate thinking and (2) poor personal integrity, that is, lacking moral qualities of excellence like honesty, trust, and commitment to promises made. But if you can integrate and master intellectual and moral excellence in your life, then you will rise to the top of your class and community. People will remember your name. Why? Because you seized your studies with excellence with a larger project or plan in mind, namely, to become a person of distinction. While many people develop and grow, few ever master virtue.

This book aims to give you a launching pad, a starting point, a compass, a practical step-by-step guide filled with hard lessons experienced and learned, observed, and researched, so that you may reach your full potential at the college and university level and beyond. In every chapter we not only include what we think the essentials are, but we also share commonly asked questions by our students and conversations shared over excellent coffee – for coffee is not an addiction, but a pleasure! The topics range from how to handle conflict to learning how to discover yourself and what you are to do with your life.

For those who have been blessed with certain privileges, resources, and successes, the opportunity to strategically build upon what has been entrusted to you also can be realized from this guide. For those of you who seek to have a "re-start," to go beyond what your friends and even family members ever imagined, we got you! A new day dawns!

"Principles for the Development of a Complete Mind:
Study the science of art. Study the art of science.
Develop your senses- especially learn how to see.
Realize that everything connects to everything else."

—Leonardo da Vinci

LIFESAVING TIPS

The Challenges of Family Support

We realize that being the first in your family to go to college or a university presents a unique set of burdens and privileges that others may not recognize. In my (Paul) family, I had to fulfill the family obligation of joining the military once I graduated from high school. While that was one of the most significant decisions I ever made, that is, serving my country as a hospital corpsman in the United States Naval Reserves for eight years, my parents were ambivalent about me attending a college or university. Instead of pursuing undergraduate and graduate degrees, they wanted me to commit to the military. Consequently, my service in the military helped provide funding for me to earn an undergraduate degree and generate inspiring experiences! My parents never demanded I pursue higher levels of education other than receive a high school diploma. Why? To them, college was optional and not necessary.

But for other families, there is an expectation that children attend and graduate from a college or university. Parents and caregivers make financial provisions for it. They travel to different institutions to explore college life. Moreover, they outline possible degree plans that best fit their giftedness, family values, and perhaps even generational commitments and obligations (e.g., family-owned business; legal practice; teaching; medicine).

In my (Raul) family, education was an expectation that was fostered early. My parents were both first-generation college students and valued education. They followed their dreams to become educators and complete their doctoral degrees. They had terrific childhood experiences but wanted to create better lives for themselves and for their children. As a result, access to educational opportunities and resources were plentiful for me growing up. That being stated, my own motivation to succeed and harness my education was entirely my decision and something I worked towards as well. Not only did I attend college full-time, for example, but I also worked full-time and remained employed throughout my college career. Therefore, regardless of levels of support, individuals must decide for themselves if they truly want to pursue education and make a difference in their own lives. It is an individualistic decision and one that entirely depends on one's goals and aspirations. There is no right answer!

For many, the academic support(s) may not exist, but other excellent and worthy emphases may be in place, such as serving the community, possessing a hard work ethic, providing financial support for family, and meeting the needs of loved ones (e.g., care for elderly; special needs).

Still, for others (like Paul's experience), they never received the knowledge to know what to do, what questions to ask, or how to put a plan together for undergraduate studies. Not knowing about admission requirements, why GPA (Grade Point Average) matters, or even what a major is, some students do what they can at school, pursue what they like such as sports, fulfilling day-to-day family responsibilities, and caring for others. While real fears may exist related to how to make ends meet, what to do in life, or even what to do right now, higher education is a foreign topic never discussed by those who know them best.

Does this sound like you? If so, chances are you are a first-generation student or you had life experiences similar to a first-generation student (i.e., a person who is the first in their family to attend college). Perhaps you were in high school and you thought, where do I go from here? You figured a job after high school was the reality you faced. Then, lo and behold, your friends start telling you that they have been accepted into certain colleges and universities! You begin to ask yourself, "What is this all about?" They ask you questions like, "What schools are you applying to? What is going to be your major? Have you received any scholarships, and if so, how much?" For me (Paul), I didn't even know what a GPA was till the latter end of the spring semester of my senior year in high school. Social utilities show images of your fellow high school students wearing shirts reflecting the colors of the college or university they will soon be attending. You, on the other hand, are about to grab your apron, uniform, or your work boots; another day, another dollar! You are thankful for what you have, but you wonder if you can do more.

Then things get even more complicated...

We have discovered that among first-generation families, relatives and extended family (e.g., grandparents) will either see or not see the need for their loved ones to attend college or a university. There is no "grandparent-shaming" in this statement. Many factors contribute to whether prior generations value or don't value an education. For some it is the mentality that "I did just fine without education; others can do the same." Indeed, they did! In contrast, others hold the belief that "I want a better life for my child/grandchild."

Their children, that is, your parents, will often share the same (or different) sentiment. However, even the loved ones that didn't believe education was needed often develop a growing awareness of the values and benefits of higher education, especially as they see you succeed. Others see it as optional. Perhaps they come to this recognition for you to have higher education, but their efforts are too late or their financial resources are limited. If your family falls under this category, love them, learn from them, and help them understand. Help them grow. But remember to respect them and where they came from. We all have our own life experiences, circumstances, and situational settings.

We learn things from everyone...

Sometimes we learn the most during the least expected moments. My (Raul) grandmother (Abuela) did not have a formal education. She left school in the third grade to help her mother in the home and to also help take care of her siblings; something that was expected of her at the time. Later on, my grandmother taught herself to read and write and became a notable poet, writing two collections of Spanish poems and writing song lyrics and compositions for singing competitions. She was instrumental in developing my love for music. She and I would often sing together to

Spanish ballads on the radio. We would sit on her front porch and ponder the existence of life together, sometimes coming up with the most ridiculous scenarios! I was fortunate to be her muse on two of her poems (poems she wrote about me). Above all, she taught me the importance of love, laughter, and being happy with what you have (and making the most of it). I learned so much from my Abuela and would try my best to visit her during my first and second years of college before she passed away. She was a vibrant woman who taught me more about life than I realized in the moment; most notably, how to be a good person, how to ignore the things that don't matter, and how to achieve the balance we all need to succeed. The moral of my story is to find those people in your life that you look up to and continue to spend time with them. Their time on this earth is short, and even though they may not tell you they miss you, they do. You make their day when you contact them and make plans to see them! Moreover, your families want to see you succeed. They may not have had the same opportunities you have but they definitely want you to have a better shot than they did, regardless of their understanding of the importance of education.

In summary, you recognize the value of higher education – that's why you are here with us! You long to go; you need to go! Your family either understands or they don't understand – that's OK. You (or your family) may be uncertain about the financial ramifications of higher education. Many families are at a loss on how to pay for college or won't help as much as they could because they see it as a personal choice among other competing options. So, as I (Paul) experienced, you are mostly on your own.

To be sure, these family tensions are common. You are not alone! Even if you feel alone, there are thousands of students who have chosen to do something about it. You can do the same as well! It is not an issue of being better than those who have not earned degrees. No, it is about personal achievement, advancement in education, and finding new ways to contribute to your family and community!

Here's what you can do:

First, ask for parental support in whatever way they can give it to you. Visit with your high school counselor and favorite teachers. Explain that you are a "first-generation" student (if you are) and need to have practical information to help you decide how to get into a college and university, ask what terms you need to know (e.g., syllabus), and what benefits come from graduating from a college or university. Loved ones may need to be informed why you want to earn an undergraduate degree. Resources like *Thinking with Excellence* are aimed to assist you to achieve your full potential!

Visit with those who are attending a college and university. Learn from them. Visit university and colleges as soon as possible and as early as possible-even if by yourself. Why? For the experience and for answers to your questions. Register for a campus visit over phone or online. Let them know in advance that you are coming. Set up an appointment with an admissions counselor. Attend special events held by colleges and universities (e.g., "Open House", "Showcase Saturday") that provide information on how they can assist you (e.g., financial aid), what they require for application materials, and what opportunities lie before you – if accepted. **Timing is critical** for financial assistance; know the deadlines! Colleges and universities only have so much funding set aside for scholarships. Therefore, you want to apply as early as possible to see if you can receive scholarship funds. Also, there are specific deadlines for grants and loans. If you are a minority, then there might be certain scholarships specifically set aside for you. If not, search the internet for possible grant giving businesses, non-profit institutions, and other organizations that are seeking to invest in future leaders–such as yourself. Moreover, grants, loans, and scholarships are available to qualified students. See if you qualify! Those qualifications could be varied. Lastly, even if family members cannot support you, there are resources available. But you must be timely about finding out what they are, how to apply for them, and other additional information needed that might be helpful to you. Do not wait until the last moment to see what funds are available.

I (Paul) used the military to support my education financially; the dividends from the decision to join the armed forces were exponential. My parents helped where they could. I worked at two hospitals, a grocery store, and a nursing home throughout my undergraduate years. Other people came around and blessed me in the most unexpected ways. When I graduated with my Ph.D., four degrees total, my parents could not have been more proud of my academic accomplishments; they didn't even have to say a word; you could see it beaming from their faces.

Experiencing Culture Shock

"I've always felt that if you back down from a fear, the ghost of that fear never goes away. It diminishes people."

—HUGH JACKMAN

At some point early on in your college experience – whether you're just embarking on the journey, resuming it, starting over even if you are a first-generation student or not – you will experience some form of culture shock. It may be due to cultural differences or the simple fact that you are beginning a new experience. Your brain will expand with a wide array of knowledge; you will encounter growing pains. This is a typical experience that most people will go through. The culture shock you experience will be directly related to many factors, including the distance away from home, different distinctions in the people who surround you, and differences in your surroundings. The simple act of moving to a new town, in general, can generate anxiety, foster loneliness, and even stoke underlying or tacit fears. The important thing to remember is that this is a learning experience and a time to flourish. Embrace the moment and learn from it.

When I (Raul) went to pursue college, it was 2 hours away from home. I was in a new city and in an entirely new environment. After a few days of living the dorm life and adjusting to my new classes, I began to experience culture shock and homesickness. During those moments, I found calling home and visiting with relatives in the town where I was attending school helped me tremendously. When I finally had the chance to visit home, I took a weekend and visited with my family and, it was a nice reprieve. My parents also were able to come up and visit me on several weekends during my first year, which was an excellent opportunity for me to continue to grow. Those moments were impactful in a fantastic way. Over time, my culture shock lessened, and I became more familiar with my surroundings. I became more active on my university campus and focused on my studies. Even though I was more of an introvert by nature, I made friends and "put myself out there" to become more involved with my new community.

> "We do not exist for ourselves alone, and it is only when
> we are fully convinced of this fact that we begin to
> love ourselves properly and thus also love others."
>
> —Thomas Merton

Special Message for Older Adult Learners

For those of you who are older adults pursuing a formal education for the very first time or who are returning to college to complete a degree for career goals, fulfill a life-long dream, or to uphold promises made years ago, or perhaps to gain a certain level of "respect" where you are employed, the culture shock may be overwhelming. Unlike many younger college and university students, you have a myriad of other responsibilities to shoulder such as children of your own, an aging spouse, or grandchildren to love. You have long-term commitments, responsibilities to uphold, stressors younger people can only imagine, and aches and pains to bear.

The culture shock may even involve clothing, clichés, and conversations. You may have the feeling, and it may repeatedly happen, that you are a "fish out of water," an "imposter," and even "inadequate." Coupled with the bags, drags, and sags we are all developing, you look at the syllabus for the very first time and you think, "There is no way! I don't belong here!"

We understand. We professors age as well. Our lives are not carefree, centered on studies, social life, and student traditions. The quest for connecting with younger generations of students can become exponentially difficult. There is much we can learn from one other, however!

If you take some time to look around, you will likely see greater age diversity than you realize. More and more adult learners are returning to school. You might also recognize that the classmates around you that are younger share the same fears, anxiety, hopes, and dreams. There are all sorts of students from all stages of life taking classes for a wide array of reasons. The diversity is beautiful!

> "Getting over a painful experience is much like crossing monkey bars.
> You have to let go at some point in order to move forward."
>
> —C. S. Lewis

What will help you, the older adult learner, to make a successful transition includes the following. First, while you can't let go of all your responsibilities, look at your daily schedule and see what you can cease from doing, even if for a season. Second, lean upon your network of family and friends; you will need them. Third, ease into the college and university life. In other words, don't rush to take a full-load if it is not necessary. Fourth, you can significantly add to the educational classroom setting; younger students need to hear from you! In fact, your experiences shared, multiple roles experienced, and abilities mastered give the classroom teaching process a specific richness not found when all the students are of the same level in both age and experience. Regularly meet with your professors and strategize together given classroom discussions that can be pursued, building off of each other's experiences. Fifth, take advantage of opportunities to engage younger students. Not only will you learn from them, but they will also learn from you. Most students actually welcome the chance! Sixth, if you haven't already, consider attending a college or university that has a flexible teaching schedule given the challenging roles you are fulfilling and responsibilities you are carrying. And lastly, develop friendships wherever you attend school. Be intentional!

Whether you are young or old, it is important to remember that the college and university experience is an adjustment process. Feelings of culture shock will pass with time. You will thrive and learn from it if you let yourself do so!

"Courage is a special kind of knowledge: the knowledge of how to fear what ought to be feared and how not to fear what ought not to be feared."

—David Ben-Gurion

CHAPTER ONE

Three Habits to Master in Everyday Life

"People almost invariably arrive at their beliefs not on
the basis of proof but on the basis of what they find attractive."

—BLAISE PASCAL

Master your habits or they will master you!

Thinking with excellence begins with habitually mastering three questions, no matter where you are, what you are doing, or wherever you are going. A habit is to think, feel, desire, and act in such a way that you do not consciously will to do it; you just do it! Therefore, the three habits you want to acquire are to think like a detective, read to understand, and learn the art of conversation.

Think like a Detective

In every course of study, situational setting, and season of life consistently ask these three questions to the extent that these questions become habituated into your life:

What do I see? (The Power of Careful Observation).[2] Make as many obser-vations as you possibly can (and then make more) before you move to interpretation. Avoid making premature judgments...allowing the will to rush ahead of your mind. In other words, resist making premature judg-ments until you have made every observation possible (especially with others). Careful observation is needed for accuracy. Think of yourself as a most excellent detective, collecting as much information as you can about a situation and then interpreting that information.

What does it mean? (Reasonable Interpretation). Carefully examine the context to help you understand its meaning. Look for things related to it. Context is important because you don't want to miss anything related to the author or speaker's intended meaning. This is important in all areas, especially the classroom as you make notes and study for exams.

Application-What is its significance? How, when, and where is this appli-cable? Is it truly workable? Is it significant? Is it worthwhile? How does it promote intellectual and moral excellence and contribute to the true good of others?

Not only do you want to think like a detective, but also the second habit you want to acquire diligently is in the area of required and recommended readings (whether articles, books, charts, discussion boards, magazines, newspapers, and even creative assignments). Similar to Chall's reading stages that have been utilized to explain reading development in young children, do not merely read for the sake of reading, but also read to under-stand and to learn![3]

Read to Understand

If you can't remember what you've read, then it is likely you didn't read the work; you merely looked at it or "skimmed" it. Want to change from that

---

[2]   Insights of observation, interpretation, and application are adapted from Howard Hendricks and William D. Hendricks, *Living By the Book: The Art and Science of Reading the Bible*, new ed. (Chicago, IL: Moody Press, 2007).

[3]   Jeanne Chall, *Stages of Reading Development* (New York: McGraw Hill, 1983) 10-24.

mind-numbing approach and a waste of time? Read like you are reading a love letter from someone with great interest. Read with the same intensity and attention as you would when you read about your favorite subject.

> "Study without desire spoils the memory,
> and it retains nothing that it takes in."
>
> —Leonardo da Vinci

Conquer your reading with questions. Like a good conversation with someone, bombard your reading with WH questions: Who? What? When? Where? Why? How? To what extent? Begin the questioning with your book title. Second, turn to the table of contents and pay particular attention to the chapter titles. Turn each chapter title into questions using the WH questions mentioned above. Third, gain familiarity with the sources used in a bibliography or works cited page. Prime yourself by asking whether you have any prior knowledge on the subject. Search for some prior experience or learning that you can link to the reading. Keep asking yourself these questions to understand what you are reading: What is the overarching thesis, message, central argument, or main idea of this book? How did the author come to that conclusion? In other words, what evidence does the author have to support this thesis? Why is this significant to know? Remember, your goal is to get into the mind of the author in the same way that you attempt to do when you are reading a love letter. To fully understand and learn the material, you must access that same place of interest and emotion.

Understand the meaning of important words, names, and locations, and movements used. Look for words that are emphasized, repeated, related, alike, and unalike. When you discover them, highlight them, write them down, look them up; understand what they mean. The more you say the word and the more you write it down, the easier it will be to learn it. If you see a particular name, movement, or location emphasized or reoccurring, do some research and find out who they are or what it is. Why is this particular word relevant to the author?

"True life is lived when tiny changes occur."

—LEO TOLSTOY

Don't travel down rutted roads in your reading. There is a tendency to travel down rutted roads in our observations and in our thinking. Therefore, to avoid those down-trotted paths, change the way you read! Read silently. Read aloud. Read with others. Read thoughtfully, patiently, critically, meditatively, purposefully, microscopically, imaginatively, repeatedly, attentively, acquisitively, and selectively.

Don't be fearful about reading! Read only one chapter at a time. Instead of thinking about how big the book is, focus only on conquering a chapter each time you read. Consequently, you will experience fulfillment if your goal seems more manageable. Don't let the size of the book intimidate you. The question is not how many pages you read but did you understand what you read?

Know yourself! Like a successful person in sports, you must train with the goal of excellence in mind. Therefore, if at all possible, read when you are most "alive." In other words, read when you are at your best moments physically, mentally, and emotionally. While this may prove difficult given other demands, try not to study when you know you will be exhausted, fatigued, sleepy, or not very alert. Remember, small pockets of time go a long way! You may only have 15-20 minutes to read during an optimal moment, but that is time well spent. If you read a little bit every day, then you will have less to do later.

Watch what and when you eat and drink. Be careful when you eat and how much you eat. Avoid large portions, high sugar, and high carbs before or during your reading time. If you don't, then you will not be able to think or focus well; your reading goals likely will be short-lived. Always stay hydrated; start each day with two glasses of water. In fact, drink lots of water on a daily basis and get plenty of rest. Yes, this is sometimes easier said than done, but you will feel better and see improvement.

Want to be a reader of excellence?
Check out Mortimer J. Adler's *How to Read a Book*.

Learn The Art of Conversation

In addition to mastering three important life thinking skills, always asking (1) what do I see, (2) what does it mean, and (3) what is its significance – as well as mastering reading to understand and learn (not merely reading to read)–you also want to learn the art of conversation. Conversation is a delicate interplay between two people. It is a subset of communication in that communication can be viewed as the umbrella term for disclosing information. But conversation is much more critical and the ultimate goal in communication. It is an exchange of information, an interchange of sharing between two or more people. When two or more people are face-to-face, a conversation not only involves components of speech and language (vocal quality, speech, grammar, syntax) but also includes eye contact, dialect, inflection, prosody, and body language (social communication and pragmatics). Interestingly, about five minutes after meeting someone new it is incredible what you can learn:

1   What matters most to them

2   What they are currently struggling with

3   How they manage to cope with their struggles

4   If they are happy with their family or social life

5   How the majority of their time is spent and if they love or resent it

If you want to think with excellence, then you must master the art of conversation. Why? We are the product of thousands of conversations. Pause, and let that sink in! Reflect upon the people who have influenced, informed, and instructed your life. Ask yourself this question: When I am conversing with others, how am I influencing, informing, and instructing *THEIR* lives? We all impact others. What influences do you want to impart on the world? Therefore, here are some essentials to the art of conversation.

Actively listen

Don't think about something else or allow yourself to become distracted. Avoid the tendency to think merely about responding to a conversational partner or setting up your next question in advance while they are speaking. Listen to what they have to say. Make eye contact. Focus on what they are saying. Put the smartphone/technology away!

Ask good questions

Ask questions of clarification like "What do you mean?" How did you come to that conclusion?" "Tell me more." Moreover, ask questions with purpose that will advance the conversation. Acknowledge the person's feelings and show them that you are interested in what they are saying.

Summarize

Conversation is not complete until you have contributed. But when you do speak, summarize, summarize, and summarize! No need to give unnecessary details. Don't wear people out with your words!

Observe

Watch your body language and the body language of other people. Make eye contact. Study their posture. Watch your words: Avoid using words repeatedly and word fillers like "um," "like," "and," and "ah." Profanity, while perhaps fun to use to make particular points, is also unnecessary to converse effectively. Lastly, when you do observe, don't invade personal body space. When a person invades personal body space, it can be quite distracting. Remember, you can't predict the other person's communication skills and how they interact, but you *CAN* lead by example!

Referee conversation (if needed)

Once again, conversation is not complete until there is an exchange and you have contributed. But if the person will not allow you to engage, attempt to referee the conversation by making a verbal agreement. Use non-verbal gestures to help you create a pause whereby you can offer a verbal agreement. Take your turn according to the agreement. If they refuse to allow you to speak or do not listen to you when you do speak, then let them finish and move on.

Reflect

Afterward, consider the following questions: what did you learn from this conversation? What can you do to be a better conversationalist? If you need to interact with and converse with that person again, what can you do differently next time to make it a more meaningful and better conversational experience?

Respect

In order to have enriching conversations that hopefully lead to meaningful relationships, make sure your overall hygiene (e.g., breath; body order, cleanliness) is pleasant. Dress appropriately. This cannot be emphasized enough. As the saying goes: in the workplace, you should dress not for the job you have but for the type of job you desire to have. The same can be said for pursuing education and friendships. Do not allow your clothing choices to be a distraction to others, not only in conversation but also in the classroom. Moreover, exercise! Find a program or regimen that is appropriate for you; whether it is a cardio/weight routine or an occasional walk. Stay active. Your future self will thank you. Your mind will stay alert and your overall health will improve. Respect your body.

A discussion on respect would not be complete without addressing respect towards conversational partners. When you converse with others, they may sometimes tell you interesting or "juicy" details about their lives or the lives of people you know (or do not know). Avoid at all costs the temptation to gossip or talk negatively about people. It has been said that the way people talk about others to you is how they will talk about you to others. Keep your conversations meaningful and positive as much as possible. Sure, everyone has bad days. In those moments; however, try your best to find something to be grateful for and be the influence you wish to receive from others!

Conclusion

If you master these three skills of excellence, namely, (1) think like a detective, (2) read to understand, and (3) learn the art of conversation, you will step into a larger world not only in the way you think but also in the way you live. What you will experience is a textured richness, a dynamic interplay between your identity and development, what you are and who you will become, and where you are and where you will go. You will see your surroundings in a new way. Friendships will grow. Relationships will be made. You will have a greater sense of belonging. The opportunity is before you. Thinking with excellence begins here! Are you ready for the challenge to become more than you ever thought possible?

"Character may be manifested in
the great moments, but it is made in the small ones."

—Sir Winston Churchill

LIFESAVING TIPS

"How Can I Avoid Loneliness?"

Adjusting from high school, full-time work, or military into college and university life can be a significant change, bring about significant challenges, and even generate loneliness. But at the same time, this new setting can create new opportunities, bring forth transformative experiences, and connect you to other students that may engender some of the most significant friendships you will ever know. So, for some, this transition to college and university life is riddled with challenges. For others, this opportunity is a "second chance," a "do-over," a "rebirth" from past emotional baggage, blunders, and bullies. Whether you are an extrovert or introvert, here are ten steps to alleviate the threat of loneliness your first semester and beyond:

First, capitalize on your college and university life within the first week of the fall semester. After the fall semester begins, friendship circles will form. Students have observed that it is often difficult (but not impossible) to get into those groups by the end of the first month of school life.

Second, if you are living on campus, move into the residential halls and apartments at the same time as your classmates. You will share the experience of moving in together, which is likely to promote opportunities for making friends. Moreover, you can offer to help others move in which will generate more possibilities.

Third, walk through the University Center or Student Center and look for advertisements posted for clubs, associations, and organizations the weekend before the semester begins. Take bulletin boards seriously as you walk from building to building. For the next two months, regularly look for announcements regarding opportunities to interact with others.

Fourth, be involved with those who share your major and minor from the very first semester you begin your studies: clubs, convocations, special gatherings, lectureships, and "brown-bag" (bring your own lunch) discussions, and research opportunities. Being involved with the college, division, or department of your major and minor will promote occasions to interact with those who have like-minded interests.

Fifth, initiate friendships! Do not wait for people to come to you! Go to them and introduce yourself. In other words, you create the possibilities.

Sixth, ask meaningful questions. When you introduce yourself to others, ask good questions and look communicative partners directly in the eye. Good eye contact shows intent, interest in the topic, and promotes a sense of confidence, even if it is not fully developed.

Seventh, be a good listener. Rarely do people listen. But if you can thoughtfully listen to what others say and ask good questions in response (we cannot overemphasize this enough), then you will offer something most people do not encounter on a daily basis, namely, one who actually listens to what they have to say. As you thoughtfully listen to others, you will develop credibility. Remember, being a good listener also means not talking too much!

Eighth, commit your will to the *true good* of others. If you can anticipate, meet, and exceed the needs of others with the energy, gifts, resources, and talents you possess, then you will be amazed how loneliness is alleviated. For example, create an opportunity for a study group to master testable material. In other words, go beyond yourself to meet the needs of others.

Ninth, be yourself but be mindful of how you dress and present yourself.

And **tenth**, know yourself. No matter your background, circumstances, or past, you possess inherent value. What are your gifts, your talents, your temperament, and leadership skills? Remain positive. You have a lot to offer to others! Don't allow yourself to succumb to loneliness.

> "If you go out looking for friends, you're going to find they are very scarce.
> If you go out to be a friend, you'll find them everywhere."

—ZIG ZIGLAR

CHAPTER TWO

How to Do Well in Any Class

"Nothing is more common than unfulfilled potential."

—Howard Hendricks

One of the hardest lessons we have learned is how to do well in our courses of study. But by learning from our mistakes, overcoming challenges, and watching how others handle the classes they take, here is what we have discovered that will not only help you do well in any class, but will also help you become one who thinks with excellence: manage the essentials, embrace the 10 maxims of excellence, and make new friendships. Know your syllabus, required readings, teacher, professor, fellow students, and yourself. Handle all forms of communication with tender care.

Master the Essentials

Carefully read your syllabus. Pro-actively bombard your syllabus with the same WH questions you will give to your reading: Who? What? When? Where? Why? To what extent? Carefully study the course objectives. Come up with a plan that will help you understand what those course objectives are and not only meet them, but also exceed them. If you master the course objectives, then you will have greater control over your final grade. Lastly, create a calendar with all your assignments due for every class. Assign a particular color for each class (e.g., biology is green; math is red; history is blue; English is yellow). Coordinate colors with the assignments. Stand back and look at what you need to complete. Create a plan. Stick with the plan! If you enrolled in an online class, we recommend checking every day to see if any announcements have been posted or emails have been received.

How Do I Study a Syllabus?

Step 1: Study Course Objectives: This will not only shed light into what the goals are in a particular course, but they are also to be your goals.

Step 2: Consider Course Guidance: What are the titles of each class meeting? What are the major themes or ideas that will be covered? This will give you insight into how the course is designed.

Step 3: Meet Deadlines: Examine the deadlines for assignments, exams, papers, and required readings. Mark them in your calendar. Keep up with your calendar.

Step 4: Adopt Policies: What are the policies for this course? What is the professor demanding? What is the university requiring?

Step 5: Know Your Professor: Know your professor's office location and office hours. What is the best way to contact the professor? Does the professor prefer email?

Step 6: Gather Materials: What books are required and recommended? Are they available in the library? Is there an e-version of the books required and recommended?

Consider making an outline of the major units of thought in your readings. As you formulate your outline from the reading, ask yourself the following question: *"What do I see?"* The more observations you make, the better your interpretation of the author's position or claim may be. Next ask, *"What does it mean?"* After you outline the author's position/claim go back and see what arguments are being provided to support that position or claim. Keep asking yourself, *"What is the issue?"* Then consider what objections can be raised against that issue, position, or claim. Lastly, what replies can be given to defend the position or claim?

Consult with your professor. You should consult your instructors as often as needed to make sure you understand the material. Do not wait until the day before a test to begin studying. Thinking with excellence implies active studying and engagement. Take advantage of your instructor's office hours.

Communicate effectively with your professor. Introduce yourself to your instructor, using the art of conversation to make a great first impression. In Western cultures, they say "the squeaky wheel gets the grease." In Asian countries, they say a variation of "the duck that quacks loudest will get shot." Find an appropriate middle ground and be respectful to your instructors. That first impression will make a lasting impact. When you email instructors, address them by "Professor," "Dr.," or "Mr./Mrs." and their last name. Be mindful of what you write in correspondence. Formal email exchange is expected and encouraged.

The following is an example of what *NOT* to do when you email your instructor. This example represents an actual email correspondence from a college student that has been received by an instructor. The name has been omitted to protect the student. The example is a very common form of email correspondence that many students who are unaware of email etiquette use. It is important to remember that there is a more formal way to address instructors. An example of what to do instead is provided. While instructors appreciate your candidness, just like there is an art to conversation there also is an art to writing an appropriate email!

Example of what *NOT* to do when emailing an instructor:

> Hey,
> So I missed class today...I overslept. What did I miss? If I missed a pop quiz I'll just make it up next time.
> kay thanks

Do this instead:

> Dear Dr. _____,
>
> I apologize for missing class today. I should have notified you before class. I have a medical condition, and when my medicine was changed this past week, it caused drowsiness that impacted my class attendance. I just wanted to let you know that I will consult with a classmate to get important notes and materials. Also, I am happy to provide you with a note from my doctor regarding my medical issue. It is my understanding that I missed a pop quiz. Please let me know if I will be allowed to make this up. Thank you so much for your understanding. I really enjoy your class and appreciate your time and attention to this email. Looking forward to the next class!
>
> Respectfully,
>
> Student

Notice in the example that, initially, the student did not address the professor properly in the greeting and had several assumptions regarding making up a quiz. Always address the professor appropriately and use full, grammatically correct sentences. Avoid as many colloquialisms (e.g., "kay") as possible until the professor's tone via email has become more informal. This will be very impactful and will engender more respect from your professor.

Respect your professor. Always be sure to respect your professor, in and outside of the classroom. Your professor is a person too with desires, dreams, blessings, and burdens. When you take advantage of a professor's office hours, don't be insensitive to the time provided or abuse generosity given. To be sure, don't disrupt or even malign the teaching objectives, information, requirements, and actual teaching process. In fact, don't argue with your professor; it has a lasting impact. Just remember this quote I (Paul) once heard from the famed prison administrator and warden of the historical Louisiana State Penitentiary (known as Angola), Burl Cain, "I will be as nice as you will allow me to be, but I will be as mean as you make me." Never disrespect your professors in public or in private; they want you to succeed. "What should I do if I feel my professor is being unfair?" If you have a problem with your professor, follow proper college or university policies.

Participate in class. Class participation is encouraged, especially when you do not understand a concept. Don't be afraid to raise your hand and ask for clarification on what you might think is a silly question. Chances are that other students probably have the same question and are too afraid to ask. Your professor will appreciate your willingness to participate. Even if there aren't any points associated with participation in class, stand out. You will learn more by raising your hand and getting a question wrong rather than sitting quietly. It's a remarkable thing. Your involvement in class will only add to the active experience of the group as a whole. Make the most out of the classroom experience!

"A well-educated mind will always have more questions than answers."

—HELLEN KELLER

Form study groups. Form study groups to prepare for quizzes and exams – this is so important! Make friends in class and find people that you genuinely connect with. Show up five to ten minutes early to class. While you are waiting for class to start, instead of checking social media or using your smartphone to text or call someone, put electronics away and talk to your classmates. Introduce yourself and get to know them. Build relationships and, thus, build study groups! Find at least one study partner in each class. When you are studying for a quiz or exam, "teach" your fellow classmates important concepts. We typically learn the best when we have the opportunity to teach and explain it to others. Ask each other questions and put definitions and explanations in your own words.

Sit up front. Those who sit at the front of the classroom do better on exams than those who sit in the back? Why? People in front of you have a higher chance of distracting you by their activities, mannerisms, and movements.

Moreover, being in front of the teacher cultivates more significant interest in the class. More eye contact is made. Pressure to listen and behave appropriately also is expected.

Study when you are at your best. Once again, try to read when you are at your best. If you are a "morning person," for example, then make time to study in the morning and not late at night. When you are studying, try to reduce as many extraneous distractions as possible and give it your full attention.

Know other students. Remember how important it is to form study groups? Make sure you have contact information for at least one other student from class and that you feel comfortable reaching out to this person for lecture material in case you happen to miss a class. Choose your person(s) wisely! Although you may not always know what kind of student they are, first impressions can go a long way. Try your best to find someone reliable who will take detailed notes and who feels comfortable sharing them with you. Likewise, be open to sharing in return – and do the same for them. Be a good person to others.

Practice proper "netiquette." In this day and age, there is a tendency for people to be more respectful in face-to-face situations (for the most part) rather than online forums. If you go to any online social media platform, for example, this becomes apparent when discussions involve politics, religion, or other highly charged topics. As a participant in the educational process, it is important to remember that you should strive to display the same level of respect you would in hybrid and online classes as you would in "brick and mortar" classrooms. Construct your responses to instructors and students with the same level of care as you would in an email to people you would see on a regular basis. Just because you might not see them in person doesn't mean that you should show them any less respect.

Adopt time management. Time management is essential to thinking with excellence. You must be disciplined with your time. If you study a little bit every day, then you will never have to do too much when an assignment is due or an exam needs to be taken. It just takes 10-15 minutes a day. What you will discover is that you will learn more than the person who crams their studies in the last moment. In fact, mastering the daily habit of studying a little bit every day will cause you to outpace even the most naturally gifted students. It is amazing how an individual's capabilities do not generate success compared to those who possess willingness, a drive within, to seize their studies, discipline to carry it out, and frequent, rich exposure to the material. An excellent detective studies the crime scene repeatedly, with tenacity, and values fresh perspectives. Do the same! Seize the moment! You will never regret studying more, being more attentive to the material, or making quality time.

Born and raised in East Texas I (Paul) was taught that the word "car" had three syllables. While I joke about my East Texas dialect, my education was adequate but not remarkable. My parents did not receive a formal education. In fact, in their day, they didn't need to pursue undergraduate or even graduate education. While higher education was helpful to many, my parents trusted the education they had received and the educational system in general to do its job. But when I personally discovered the essentials toward the end of my undergraduate program, my grades shifted from being good to great. Later, when I attended graduate school and sat around students who were more gifted than I was, who possessed more resources than I did, and who attended institutions such as Princeton University, Yale University, United States Naval Academy, University of California-Berkeley, and Texas A&M University, I experienced envy as well as insecurity (like I didn't belong there with them). Interestingly, when I took my very first semester, I found myself outpacing these same students. In fact, some of my classmates I envied the most asked me for help, specifically, how I was able to grasp the material so easily compared to them. How might you ask? Managing the essentials. You can do it as well! The question is rarely about one's capability; the issue is often one's willingness. Will you be so daring?

> "The two factors that will influence you the most in the years ahead are the books you read and the people you're around."
>
> —HOWARD HENDRICKS

10 Maxims to Follow

Not only do you want to master the essentials, but here are ten maxims (rules of conduct) we encourage you to embrace in your life in order to think with excellence! Many of us don't like rules. But if you follow these ten, then you will be amazed what you will accomplish in your studies and in life. The long-term goal would be that these rules would become habits of excellence in your life. A habit is to think, feel, desire, and act, in such a way that you don't consciously will to do it; you just do it. The rules of conduct can become part of your identity, shaping who you are in the most amazing ways.

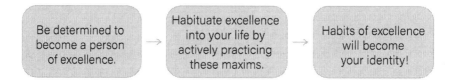

1   **Be focused!** Your energy, time, and discipline need to be dedicated to becoming the very best. Focus on what really counts. Do not allow yourself to become diverted by trivial and unimportant things. This includes people. There are "givers" and "takers" in this world. Be careful with the "takers." They will drain the life out of you if you let them!

2   **Be holistic!** Pro-actively make decisions and pursue interests in your daily life that will assist you in obtaining success. Your resources must always be redirected to your goal.

3   **Be undivided!** Do not separate one area of your life from another. Pursuing opposing interests may marginalize your success because it divides up your energy, time, resources, and attention.

4   **Be determined!** Academic progress is challenging, time-consuming, and demanding. Meet every demand with a determination for excellence. Learn from your mistakes. Pick yourself up when you fail and press on!

5   **Be resilient!** Do not give up. You will perhaps fail some time or another during your program. View failure not as a detriment but as an

opportunity to learn. The most successful people have failed numerous times. Keep your chin up! You may even become depressed from the critical feedback you receive from your professors and peers. When those times arise, and they will for most if not all, you must pick yourself up over-and-over again. Remember, accomplishing the goal is worth facing seemingly insurmountable obstacles.

6   **Be sacrificial!** Purposefully let go of those things that will hinder your success. Willfully discard every hindrance and degenerative influence that will keep you from achieving your goal with a passion for excellence. Routinely examine your life and see what is encouraging or discouraging you from reaching excellence.

7   **Be healthy!** Realize, as Aristotle observes in his famous, seminal work, *Nicomachean Ethics*, that one area of your life impacts all other areas, whether intellectual, physical, or moral. Take very tender care of your mind, soul, and body. You need to strive to be holistically healthy – for if you are not mentally, physically, and spiritually healthy, then you may easily develop fatigue, inner angst, regret, and disappointment. Any of these may cause you to waiver in the completion of your goals. Remember, adequate rest is one of the best things you can do for yourself.

8   **Be supported!** Cultivate a network of people who will encourage you to succeed! Develop relationships with peers who share your same aspirations for achieving success.

9   **Be excellent!** Successful students realize the importance of cultivating a disposition, i.e., an inner character, which desires intellectual and moral excellence. Seek to desire excellence. Aristotle encourages us to do deeds of excellence until excellence becomes habitual in our personhood.

10   **Be balanced!** Learn how to balance "having fun" with "hard work." Don't ignore those opportunities to relax or play hard. In fact, pursue them! But do not allow those occasions to displace your studies. Remember, learning is pleasurable!

These ten rules of conduct or maxims, if inscribed into your identity by actively practicing them, will help propel you towards excellence that will last a lifetime. But you have to be intentional, consistent, and mindful; this is your long-term project that must be practiced in moment-by-moment living. Like lifting weights in a gym, *how* you think is just as important as what you think.

"How you think when you lose determines how long it will be until you win."

—G. K. CHESTERTON

Manage the essentials and habituate these ten maxims into your life. What else can you do? Make genuine friendships. How?

How to Plan for Making Genuine Friendships

One of the most life-changing aspects of your educational experience is making authentic friendships. Aristotle points out that there are three types of friendships: (1) friends of utility (students who complete a task together), (2) friends of pleasure (students who mutually enjoy a sporting event, social gathering, or club), and (3) intimate friends (students who share commitment to each other's true good). It is a universal sociological and psychological fact that everyone desires friendships; we are social creatures.

Why are developing friendships necessary for thinking with excellence? At our core, we need one another. For example, there is strength in community, an iron sharpening process. Without a community to support us, we are prone to traveling down rutted roads in our thinking, developing misperceptions, making premature judgments, and not looking from the eyes of others (putting ourselves in other people's perspectives).

Making genuine friendships requires more than just taking someone out to lunch or talking sports, movies, or clothing. A genuinely close friend is the kind of friend you can talk to about anything and everything without competition, fear, embarrassment, betrayal, or judgment; the kind of friend who loves you as you really are (or at least in spite of it).

"A Friend loves at all times...

There is a friend who sticks closer than a brother"

—PROVERBS 17:17A; 18:24

Pursuing friendships may be awkward at first, and definitely requires hard work, but it is well worth it! Here's a recommended step-by-step plan to make great friendships that may last a lifetime:

1   Initiate the code of "invitation." Think of regular activities you and your new friend can do together. Invitation involves regular and frequent time (every once in a while, invitations alone "ain't gonna cut it!").

2   Initiate the code of "authenticity." Trust, transparency, and vulnerability are the "stuff" in which true friendships are made of. This is how you go beyond the *clichés*, the superficial levels of friendship, and instead move forward towards the friendships where the other person accepts you for who you are. To be sure, you don't have to share everything but you definitely want to be authentic. Authenticity builds bridges of friendships.

3   Practice "personal vulnerability." If you stiff-arm your friend when one starts to get too close, that person will receive the message and withdraw, unless that person is particularly secure and committed. But please know most people are not secure because of the realistic possibility of rejection. Rejection is painful. In fact, there are studies where researchers have found that rejection is perceived and processed as actual pain.[4] In every social circle there are people who are hurting. But a real friendship can be a healing "salve" to many of our problems. Therefore, anticipate the possibility of pain. Practice authenticity and personal vulnerability in conversation. In fact, if an excellent friendship is to be developed, authenticity and vulnerability will be demanded.

---

[4]   See Ethan Kross, Mark G. Berman, Walter Mischel, Edward E. Smith, and Tor D. Wager, "Social Rejection Shares Somatosensory Representations with Physical Pain." *Proceedings of the National Academy of Sciences of the United States of America*, 2011.

4   Practice "commitment": Let your "yes" be *yes* and your "no" be *no*. Do not be *that* person who refuses to commit till the last moment, who remains hopeful of possible alternatives, or who struggles with indecisiveness. Your friendships will be limited if you are unable to keep your promises, too busy with other responsibilities, or if you expect people to read your mind. Follow through with commitments made! Also, do not under-communicate or people will likely misread you and pursue friendships elsewhere. If you want real friends, then you must invest in them and they must be allowed to invest in you.

5   **Anticipate, meet, and exceed the needs of your friendship.** Simply put, anticipate your friend's needs. Meet those needs. Relationships should be "give AND take." Exceed those needs with intellectual and moral excellence.

Conclusion

This chapter features critical skills and considerations in order to perform well in any class. There are many paths to succeeding in the classroom and, while this list is not exhaustive, we believe that it does provide an excellent foundation for academic performance in higher education. Study what is required of you in your class (e.g., know your syllabus and required readings) and invest in a professional relationship with your instructor (one that is respectful). Show the same level of respect towards your fellow students, and don't forget about respecting yourself! So remember, manage the essentials, embrace the ten maxims of excellence, and make new, genuine friendships!

> "Resolved, never to do anything, which I should be
> afraid to do, if it were the last hour of my life."
>
> —JONATHAN EDWARDS

LIFESAVING TIPS

"I Can't Understand the Material! What Can I Do?"

When professors start probing *why* students are struggling they are likely to discover students are not adequately studying the material in preparation for class lecture. Class lectures presuppose, and rightfully so, that students are actively preparing themselves before each class lecture begins. Thus, the best key to unlock the understanding of difficult material is repeated exposure; in the same way an athlete trains for competition. See, the professor, a coach, is assuming students, like good athletes, are preparing themselves. Likewise, class time may be likened to an athletic event. In order to do well, practice, eat nourishing meals, sleep well, and practice more! In other words, the same type of focus used by good athletes is needed for understanding difficult material in the classroom.

Like poor athletes, inadequate preparation is usually symptomatic of a more significant problem. This can be reduced to five major possibilities: (1) students don't know how to study; (2) poor time management; (3) the lack of desire to even learn the material – if the material doesn't come easy, they don't want to learn it; (4) they only give their "leftovers" to what matters most. In other words, their best energy, resources, and time were spent on other things. Sometimes even what is "good" can be an enemy of what is "best." (5) Students are experiencing personal, weighty problems (e.g., home-life is a war zone; problems in relationships; addictions in areas like alcohol, drugs, gaming, and porn; parents are divorcing; suffering and death of loved ones).

Remember these essential tips: (1) sit near the front of class (less distraction); (2) read a little bit every day and you will never have to read too much at the last moment; (3) introduce yourself to the professor at the start of the course and regularly visit, asking good questions from reading.

"It's fine to celebrate success but it is more
important to heed the lessons of failure."

—Bill Gates

"I Failed My Class! What Should I Do Differently?"

When a student fails an exam, assignment, or class, it is not merely an awkward experience for the student, but it is also one that grieves us professors. We want to see our students succeed with excellence! Therefore, when students meet with us (which we highly encourage), our earnest hope is that they will translate failure into a motivating tool to greater success. Is this even possible? Not only have we experienced failure ourselves, but we also have seen some of our best students take ownership of their own failure. They recognized their problems of time management, lack of weekly preparation, writing poor papers, and cramming for an exam. The students who rose to the very top of the class from experiences of failure also seized something many students do not, namely, they proactively embraced wisdom. Translating failure into practical skills of success enabled them to do the following:

1   Turn practical mistakes into practical lessons (they learn from their past);

2   Exchange bad habits for habits of excellence (they know how to improve);

3   Have a true estimate about who they are and what they can do (they know who they are);

4   Choose the path that will lead to the highest educational transformative experience; the easiest route is usually not the best path (they choose to struggle to become great);

5   Value friendship over self-promotion (they know the power of community);

6   Pursue what matters most (they have the right priorities);

7   Understand the relationship between thought and action (they know the importance of consistency);

8   Learn from others (they observe and reflect upon what they receive);

9   Make opportunities to translate theoretical lessons from studies into living (they know where to go);

10 Ask questions and actively search for answers (they know how to think with excellence).

The question is rarely capability; the answer is always willingness.

"I Am Bilingual; I Speak Another Language Other Than English More Proficiently. What Can I Do To Succeed In Class When There Is A Language Barrier?"

First – bilingualism is a gift! Several studies point to the importance of fostering native language growth and development alongside second language development.[5] Maintaining our native language and the communicative experiences with our families and friends is so important. Embrace your heritage and culture...and differences and celebrate them! Learning another language can be challenging, but the rewards of being bilingual (or multilingual) are great. For example, speakers of other languages are needed in most career settings. Language is a valuable skill that can take you many places in life.

Now that we have stressed the importance and respect you should be given for speaking another language more fluently, here are seven tips and suggestions for excelling in the classroom if you are experiencing some challenges with the language barrier:

---

[5]   Ellen, Bialystok, "Second-language acquisition and bilingualism at an early age and the impact on early cognitive development." Revised edition, *Encyclopedia on Early Childhood Development* [online], eds. R.E. Tremblay, R. G. Barr, and R. Peters (Montreal, Quebec: Centre of Excellence for Early Childhood Development, 2008): 1-4 at *http://www.childencyclopedia.com/documents/BialystokANGxp_rev.pdf*. Retrieval date: 26 July 2018.

1   **Inform your instructor** (either through email or in person) that you are a second language learner and you want to do well in the class. Email may seem easier (e.g., online language translation software) but in person is always more personable and encouraged if you are able to do so. Remember to use online language translation software with caution as many things get "lost in translation." Have someone who is fluent in English read over your work/emails prior to sending them to make sure what you intended to convey was documented appropriately.

2   **Form a good relationship with a classmate** who can be a study partner and who can help supplement notes. Perhaps a friend/classmate is interested in learning your native language. The two of you may be able to teach one another something new!

3   **Record the lectures.** Ask your instructor if you can record the lectures – highly recommended. This will allow you not only to practice listening to English but will also provide documentation for you to refer back to your notes and expand upon them.

4   **Write notes in both English and your native language.** Infuse both of your languages together. Several studies point to bilingualism as being two systems that interact with one another. Several words in English and Spanish, for example, are cognates or written the same way but pronounced differently (e.g., animal; debate; social). Continue learning in both and use your native language as a support for your second language.

5   **Sit at the front of the class.** This may seem very frightening, especially if you are learning English as a second language; however, it will keep you focused and reduce background noises and distractions.

6   **Take additional English classes.** If given the opportunity, take other courses in English and/or immerse yourself in more opportunities for learning language. While immersion is considered to be the best way to learn a language, several additional opportunities, such as computer software, social apps, etc., exist for continued learning. Find the right fit and balance for you!

7   **Take a deep breath!** You are a superstar! Most people would find it challenging to learn a new language, especially later in life. The more you practice and allow yourself to grow in learning, the better you will become. Never feel ashamed! You are doing an extraordinary thing! Many bilingual children in school often face challenges as well and are often over-identified for special education services, even though they are following a typical acquisition of a second language[6]. Researchers estimate that it takes anywhere from 5-7 years to master a second language academically[7]. That may seem like a long time, but you have the skills and the knowledge to succeed!

> "Don't leave this world without giving it your all."
>
> —TUPAC SHAKUR

---

6   Prezas, R. F. and Jo, A. "Differentiating language difference and language disorder: Information for teachers working with English language learners in the schools. *Journal of Human Services: Training, Research, and Practice* 2 (2017), Article 2.

7   Kohnert, K. and Bates, E. "Balancing bilinguals II: Lexical comprehension and cognitive processing in children learning Spanish and English" in *Journal of Speech, Language, and Hearing Research* 45(2002): 347-359.

CHAPTER THREE

Relationship Thinking: Know How One Thinks

"Every story is informed by a worldview."

—Brian Godawa

Thinking with excellence will take on a textured, life-changing richness if you supplement your studies with worldview analysis. Why? Everyone possesses a worldview. If you truly want to understand the people around you, come to know how they think and perceive everything, including who they are, then know their worldview. Likened to a computer operating system, a person's worldview is the most essential fact of a person. It's also an excellent tool for assessing possible interpersonal relationships. But what *IS* a worldview? Understanding your own worldview is half the battle. Making sure your worldview is built upon the most significant foundations possible (justification) is the other half and will only aid you in your quest to think with excellence.

What is A Worldview?[8]

A *worldview* is one's habituated way of seeing and doing; the way one observes and interacts with the world, the sum-total of one's beliefs, ground floor assumptions, or conceptual conscious and unconscious themes by which one perceives all things. People often compare a worldview to a pair of glasses. The frames make up our fundamental assumptions, and the lenses are our biases, influences, and background or situational setting that can affect the clarity of our vision and understanding. But the illustration runs short because it can be very difficult if not painful to take one pair of assumptions off and replace them with another set.

Not All Worldviews Are Equal. To be sure, not all worldviews are the same nor possess equal explanatory power. Not all worldviews possess equal structural integrity to withstand powerful ideas, certain contexts, mesmerizing people, or weighty events that occur in one's life (e.g., tragic accident of some sort), generate values that qualitatively nourish oneself and our communities, or be able to readily handle the strains and weighty cultural, political, and social challenges of our society (e.g., hyper-partisanship; lack of civil discourse; dysfunctional homes; corruption in legal system; racism). We need to possess the most substantial support for WHY we believe what believe – even if some truth-claims appear to be more attractive than others. A truth-claim is something a person claims to be true.

Moreover, not all worldviews generate the greatest values that enrich the lives of people. Some worldviews will engender values that dehumanize people (e.g., Communism; Nazism), reducing our humanity to mere commodities or claiming that certain people or groups are sub-human. Other worldviews are not strong enough to handle the weightiness of

---

8   For the nature, value, and significance of studying worldview thinking we are indebted to William H. Halverson, *A Concise Introduction to Philosophy*, 3rd ed. (New York: Random House, New York, 167, 1972, 1976), 383-392; Nancy Pearcey, *Finding Truth* (Colorado Springs, CO: David C. Cook Publishing), 2015; Francis, A. Schaeffer, *The God Who is There*, 30th anniversary ed. (Downers Grove, IL: InterVarsity Press, 1998); James Sire, *The Universe Next Door*, 5th ed. (Downers Grove, IL: InterVarsity Press, 2009).

moral failure, the contradictions of our humanity, and the sufferings we generate by poor choices, irrational impulses, and propensities that bring out the worst in us. Blaise Pascal, a 17th century philosopher, inventor, and mathematician, summarizes the nature of our humanity quite well when he observed:

"What a Chimera is man! What a novelty, a monster, a chaos, a contradiction, a prodigy! Judge of things, an imbecile worm, depository of truth, and sewer of error and doubt; the glory and refuse of the universe."

—BLAISE PASCAL

Thus, the wounds of wickedness, the displacement of what is good for the celebration of the worst in us in the spirit of self-expression and shock value, and personal contact with evil and suffering can cause a worldview to not only fracture but also collapse.

The Problem of Pre-commitments. Other worldviews dehumanize people because of certain pre-commitments. They will ignore what is true, good, and beautiful for something less than. They willfully refuse to see what is logical, obvious, and beneficial. As a result, their worldviews possess contradictions in thinking and in living.

For example, some will deny that we possess freedom of choice because of their *willful* pre-commitment to determinism. These individuals not only make a logical mistake but also contend we are not responsible for our own moral actions; we are just dancing to our DNA. This worldview not only strips us of the freedom to choose and moral responsibility but also questions the validity of other worldviews that claim we are more than our DNA. But upon what basis can they willfully choose to evaluate other worldviews? Are their conclusions even valid or are they merely biochemical responses?

Therefore, it is critical to not only know what people believe but also what the justification is for their worldview. In other words, are these assumptions people embrace based on facts, impressions, or opinions? Even for us, we need the strongest support for why we believe what we believe even if some truth-claims appear to be more attractive to us than others. In other words, what we seek to know is what we believe and why.

Why do people believe what they believe? Following a helpful insight from James Sire,[9] we have discovered that people's justification for why they believe what they believe can be categorized into the following four areas:

1 Psychological Reasons: Personal comfort, hope, meaning, and significance.

2 Sociological Reasons: Background, community, friends, home, network of institutional authorities, parents, practices, and peers.

3 Religious/Spiritual Reasons: Religious authorities (e.g., guru, imam, pastor, priest, or shaman), gatherings, institutions, thinkers, sacred texts, and traditions.

4 Philosophical Reasons: Consistency, coherence, and completeness.

What are the justifications for what you believe? The importance of knowing what you believe and why is critical to thinking with excellence.

Know the Difference. If you know or will learn the following terms, then you will be on the path of intellectual virtue because so many people don't know the differences between assumptions, facts, impressions, and opinions.

> "Truth has been displaced as a value
> and replaced by psychological effectiveness."
>
> —ALASDAIR MACINTYRE

---

9   James Sire, "Why Should Anyone Believe Anything at all?" in D. A. Carson, ed. *Telling the Truth* (Grand Rapids: Zondervan, 2000), 93, 101.

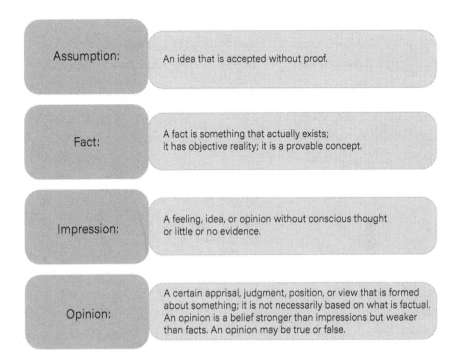

Assumption: An idea that is accepted without proof.

Fact: A fact is something that actually exists; it has objective reality; it is a provable concept.

Impression: A feeling, idea, or opinion without conscious thought or little or no evidence.

Opinion: A certain appraisal, judgment, position, or view that is formed about something; it is not necessarily based on what is factual. An opinion is a belief stronger than impressions but weaker than facts. An opinion may be true or false.

The Clarity of One's Worldview. While one person may share a set of worldview assumptions that are similar or appear to be identical to yours, the clarity of one's worldview may differ significantly. The ability to see accurately can be affected by the following:

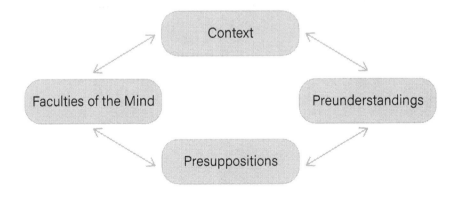

Context

Faculties of the Mind

Preunderstandings

Presuppositions

What is context? The particular circumstances or environment that form, influence, or shape the situational setting for the origin, emergence of, and/or use of a specific action, event, idea, or truth-claim.

What are pre-understandings? They are fluid-like influences that come and go. They are most evidenced in a particular context or situational setting, within interpersonal relationships, shared fellowships, and institutional settings. For example, after spending some time with a fellow student, you find yourself using similar words and tones to express things verbally. Then another person comes into your life, and you absorb this person's mannerisms, etc.

When I (Raul) was working on my graduate degrees, I lived in Kansas with relatives who used different vocabulary for everyday objects than I did. A "bag" from my world (growing up in South Texas) was now a "sack." Soda (though we tend to say a different word for all sodas in Texas) was "pop." After living in Kansas for 6 years, I can say with absolute certainty that while I still say "bag" on a regular basis, I grew to love "pop" as my term for soda and still use it to this day.

What are presuppositions? They are fixed biases that do not change unless extreme pressure is applied. These biases can take multiple forms: dislike or even disdain for a particular field of study to a person; an idea to a practice; race to religion; one's gender to one's community; economics to politics. We presuppose everyday, whether we realize it or not. In sum, biases "obscure" what we observe and are not likely to break until enough force (usually an external source) is exerted upon them.

What are the faculties of the mind? Our brains, patterns of thinking, and the nourishment of our brain can also affect the clarity of our worldview. It matters very much whether our minds are working properly.

Worldview Fracturing

When one experiences cognitive and existential tension (dissonance) to the extent that one's worldview fractures, falls apart, or is exchanged for another worldview (a better or worse one), one experiences worldview fracturing.[10] Why? Once again, not all worldviews possess the greatest explanatory power, are free from logical inconsistencies, supported by factual evidences, or are relevant, germane or pertinent to our situation, identity, and becoming. As earlier stated, some assumptions dehumanize us, taking us to places we never thought we would go, extracting the best parts of us. Dehumanizing worldviews can lead us not only on a path of chaos but a marring and scarring whereby there is little hope for recovery. Thus, the need to evaluate what people claim to be true very carefully is paramount to moral and intellectual excellence, health, and leaving a legacy worth having.

Worldviews may possess varied degrees of tension or cognitive and existential dissonance. Thus, the goal, like physical therapy, is to relieve the tension by facts, logical consistency, and evidences that address the whole person. This relief will work when your worldview harmonizes those facts, logic, and evidences together and is brought to bear in the way you actually live your life, the daily choices you make, the values your embrace, and even the pleasures you pursue. Consequently, when your worldview inherently possesses coherence, corresponding to the way things actually are, and is lived out in moment-by-moment living whereby moral and intellectual excellence becomes inscribed into your character, evidenced by your choices, and upheld by what is good, true, and beautiful, you will not only think with excellence, you will also make a life-giving difference in the most dynamic ways. There is to be no dichotomy between fact and values; they are united together into one unified worldview that addresses the complete individual (e.g., physically; emotionally; intellectually; spiritually; relationally).

---

[10] Indebted to the insights and scholarship of Francis A. Schaeffer and Nancy Pearcey on the issues related to the need for a holistic worldview, free from fact/value splits, and symptoms associated with and causes for worldview fracturing. See Francis A. Schaeffer, *The God Who is There*, 30th anniversary ed. (Downers Grove, IL: InterVarsity Press, 1998); James Sire, *The Universe Next* (Downers Grove, IL: InterVarsity Press, 2009); Nancy Pearcey, *Total Truth* (Wheaton, IL: Crossway, 2004).

Fractured worldview

Unified, coherent worldview that
corresponds with reality as it is,
possessing greatest justification possible

To be sure, worldview fracturing can be quite painful. The event can also be liberating too if one's worldview is replaced with a better one that can not only handle the problems our ever-changing society faces, but also generate values that best support our personhood and our communities.

How Can You Analyze A Person's Worldview?

You can explore your own worldview or analyze another person's worldview by exploring the answers to the following eight questions:

1 What is one's view of *God*?

2 What is one's view of *reality*?

3 What is one's view of *truth*?

4 What is one's view of *knowledge*?

5 What is one's view of *humanity*?

6 What is one's view of *ethics*?

7 What is one's view of *evil*?

8 What is one's view of *beauty*?

Thus, in casual conversation, if you can direct the conversation to the above eight questions – you can open the door to another's operating system. Their responses to these questions can provide a wealth of information regarding the eight ground-floor assumptions they embrace whereby they perceive everything else. You can discover if their worldview assumptions are supported by facts, opinions, or are mere impressions. You can discern if their justifications are psychological, sociological, religious, or philosophical and what issues might be affecting the clarity of their worldview. You can also determine if their worldviews are in tension, thus revealing something of their structural integrity. How will their worldview handle pressure from personal and social demands, painful problems, and lost dreams? But if you have trouble knowing where to begin, consider using the following:

1   Where did we come from? What are we?

2   What's gone wrong with the world?

3   What can be done to fix the problems of this world?

4   What is the good life?

5   How does one become a good person?

Conclusion

In summary, knowing the worldviews of others will not only help you understand the way they think, operate, and react the way they do, but will also challenge your own assumptions, expose your own fixed biases and moldable influences, inform your context, and even empower you to know what you believe and why. But what is most important is that *YOU* know *WHAT* you believe and *WHY*. Do your assumptions match up with reality? Do your worldview beliefs harmonize or cohere together? Are your facts and values united together in such a way that they speak to and enrich your whole person? Are you able to live out your worldview in daily living free of cognitive and existential tension? If so, you are on the path towards thinking with excellence.

"The highest and most beautiful things in life are not to be heard about, nor read about, nor seen but, if one will, are to be lived."

—Søren Kierkegaard

LIFESAVING TIPS

"How Do I Overcome My Biases?"

"Professor, I acknowledge the fact that I have biases that keep me from analyzing a truth-claim, an argument, or a proponent fairly? But what can I do to overcome my biases to be more fair in my analyses?"

In every assignment, or any aspect of life for that matter, where we have a particular debate analyzed (e.g., atheist Christopher Hitchens vs. theist William Lane Craig), there is a significant tendency for those of us with a worldview sympathetic to naturalism to agree with Hitchens and those of us with a theistic worldview to agree with Dr. Craig. But who won the debate for argumentation, evidence, rhetoric, and thoughtful illustrations is influenced if not affected by one's predisposition that involves a number of what may be described as "cognitive" biases. These biases are very likely to shape our conclusions about who won the debate before the event is even studied.

While we recognize that cognitive biases, pre-conceived notions, fluid-like influences, and even the situational setting can shape the way we observe an argument, an idea, or position, it does not have to be necessarily blinding. Here's what you can do to prevent one-sided argumentation and writing. While we are not saying we can achieve 100% pure objectivity (e.g., Cartesian certainty), we can be accurate, balanced, fair, and reasonable in our judgments if we are careful, curious, collaborative, open, and wise (e.g., patient) in our analyses.

After you have reached your tentative conclusions adopting the sevenfold criteria (which is introduced in chapter four) for evaluating truth-claims, arguments, and other worldviews, to make sure you are not one-sided in your presentation or written assignment, question your conclusions. How might you ask? The best way to examine them is through the following steps:

First Step: List Known Biases

List what known biases you possess that could possibly affect your interpretation. Those biases you list may involve those that others claim you possess.

Second Step: Probe Possible Biases

Probe your known list of biases and see if they are affecting your inquiry, the questions you raise, the methods you use, and the conclusions you make. Be honest with yourself.

Third Step: Assume the Other Person's Position

Assume an opposing worldview. In other words, try to observe and interpret things from their "set of eyes." Use their position to question your own tentative conclusions, always asking what do their truth-claims mean and how did they come to those conclusions? What are the contextual factors that contributed to their findings, benefits engendered, and problems they discovered and solutions they found?

Fourth Step: Be Honest with Yourself

While we are attracted to what we believe and quite often stubborn about our conclusions and justifications, be honest with yourself and others when it comes to a valid counter-argument.

Fifth Step: Strength from Community

Ask others to evaluate the arguments and the conclusions you made. There is strength in community; we all need one another. Listen to what people have to say. Ask them if they detect any personal biases being used in the conclusions you made. Consider your reactions to statements made. Do they reveal something about your biases?

Sixth Step: Diversity Exposes Possible Biases

Intentionally look for those whose worldview is different from your own. Ask them to evaluate the arguments presented and your conclusions made. Once again, consider how you are affected by their reactions to your findings. What does that say about you?

Seventh Step: Know Your History

Many of the truth-claims made, options explored, and opposing positions created have already been discussed in detail in historical accounts, writings, and works. It is crucial to "fact-check" yourself, as they say. You will learn fascinating things about yourself, and others, through this process. You may also encounter information that may surprise you.

Eighth Step: Look Again with a Fresh Set of Eyes

We are a society that values instant gratification. For example, social media is a platform where people jump to conclusions and comment back and forth, sometimes without considering all of the information. Before you finish your argument (including an assignment or presentation) wait at least 24 hours. After you give yourself some time, look at the arguments raised and conclusions made with a fresh set of eyes.

Ninth Step: Take Time to Re-Evaluate

Lastly, after your assignment or presentation has been graded and returned, take some time to read professor's comments, asking yourself what do others see that I am not seeing. If people repeatedly suggest or detect a certain "blinding" bias, be intentional about replacing it with what is true, factual, and what possesses moral and intellectual excellence. It is perhaps this last step that will be most crucial because you are seeking to think with excellence.

"What Should I Ask Myself When Looking For A Spouse?"

You may be wondering why this particular question is posed in this book. Interestingly, one of the most significant questions asked by students, especially over a cup of coffee at a nearby coffee bar, each and every semester, involves relationships. It may be stated that perhaps relationships become more significant in college. Many individuals meet their future spouse during this time, but it's also a consideration for the journey beyond higher education. In particular, when it comes to the person one should commit to or marry, what should one be looking for? Well, thinking with excellence cannot be underestimated when it comes to relationships, especially marriage. Here are some questions one could consider:

1 What is their worldview? This is the most important fact of a person.

2 Are they more intelligent than you? Hopefully so!

3 Do they possess habits of intellectual and moral excellence?

4 What emotional baggage do they possess?

5 What insecurities are they harboring and nuturing?

6 Psychological health?

7 If given the opportunity, study their parents; what are they like (e.g., attitude; looks; habits; propensities) and could you date/marry them?

As you explore these seven areas, know this: you can't change the person you want to marry. Instead, be asking what you are willing to live with. While you can't know everything about someone, you are always asking what you are capable of handling; this is the person you will be bringing home.

> "What are you to do with the people who
> are cursed with both hearts and brains?"
>
> —Dorothy L. Sayers

CHAPTER FOUR

Be The Hero The World Needs: Analyze Truth-Claims!

"I believe that the pursuit of truth and right ideas through honest debate and rigorous argument is a noble undertaking."

—CHARLES KRAUTHAMMER

Why do you believe what you believe? If someone were to press you, what would you say? What evidence could you offer? Likewise, how do we know if someone is right in what they believe? When people are making opposing truth-claims, how do we know which truth-claim is better than others? How do we know if something is true?

Welcome to one of the most critical tools you could ever develop if you want to think with excellence! In fact, if you can master these skills, then you will truly stand out. Coupled with personal integrity such as letting your yes be yes and no be no and fulfilling your commitments made, you will be the type of hero or heroine our world needs today.

A truth-claim is simply a statement one believes to be true. While contrary beliefs are possible, contrary truths are impossible. But in this society where people are making myriads of truth-claims, we have tools to sort out which truth-claims are worth considering over others. In fact, instead of evaluating truth-claims emotionally or from our feelings, which come and go, we have a better way! This way of evaluating truth-claims can be used with any truth-claim, whether they are celebrities or ordinary folk, teachers or students, politicians or religious leaders, young or old.

> "I've missed more than 9000 shots in my career.
> I've lost almost 300 games. Twenty-six times I've been trusted
> to take the game-winning shot and missed. I've failed over and over
> and over again in my life. And that is why I succeed."
>
> —MICHAEL JORDAN

Always Ask These Two Questions

When presented with any serious truth-claim or worldview, listen carefully and respectfully, and thoughtfully reply with good questions. Here are two questions you should consistently ask when truth-claims are being made. These two questions are applicable in any dialogue. Often times we find ourselves asking these questions when we are listening to a professor, fellow student, stranger, or friend:

1   **What do you mean by _____?** For example. Someone claims,

   "We become good by doing things." You ask the question,
   "What do you mean by *good*?" This is a question of clarification.

2   **How did you come to that conclusion?** This is a question of justification. Justification means showing or demonstrating that the truth-claim or worldview can be cogently defended or solidly substantiated.

Follow in the Footsteps of Socrates

Often considered to be the father of philosophy in western thought and culture, Socrates (469/470-399 BC), who was an amazing sculptor artist and respected soldier, mentored Plato, who mentored Aristotle. But after an interesting event whereby the famous Oracle at Delphi affirmed that no one was wiser than Socrates, he sought to dispel this truth by asking leading authorities, experts, and leaders in Athens questions about their respective fields, positions, and occupations. What Socrates came to discover is that the ordinary citizens were much more intelligent than those who ruled over them. Unfortunately, when he removed these masks of self-deception, disturbing the status quo of authority, it cost him his life in 399 BC. How he evaluated people became known as the Socratic Method. You can do the same even in everyday conversation! Be the Socrates our society needs! All you need to do is (1) be a good listener, (2) ask good questions, and (3) practice civility (be respectful, polite, and non-irrational).

> "There is only one way to avoid criticism:
> Do nothing, say nothing, and be nothing."
>
> —ARISTOTLE

Step 1: You focus on a keyword that needs analysis.
For example, "God does not exist because of the problem of evil."

Step 2: In an earnest disposition of learning you ask for a definition of that keyword. For example, "I apologize, but I am not understanding what you mean. May I ask a question? What is your definition of God?"

Step 3: A definition is given.
For example, "God is a supernatural being."

Step 4: Analyze the answer given by asking questions that uncover non-justified assumptions, impressions, opinions, and other weakness such as:

a How did you come to that conclusion?

b What evidence do you have for that definition?

c What examples do you have?

d What are counter-arguments to your definition?

e What would be alternative definitions?

f What are the strengths and weaknesses of your definition?

g Why is *THIS* the best definition?

h What are counter-arguments to your definition? What are the consequences that follow from this definition? What type of consequences?

i How does this definition unpack itself in the way we live?

Step 5: In dialogue a modified definition is proposed.
For example, "God is the Sum-Total of His Infinite Perfections."

Step 6: Repeat steps 4 and 5 (perhaps several times).

Step 7: The expert admits one's incorrect or insufficient understanding, ends conversation, or turns the conversation to someone (or something) else. The ideal goal is to continue this approach until understanding is advanced, improved, or rejected.

This is one of the most significant approaches used in the classroom and the courtroom. You can strengthen your competence in doing the Socratic Method when you engage friends or strangers in everyday conversation. These skills are wide-ranging: online discussions; corporate meetings; counseling situations; interviews; papers; speeches.

But the Socratic Method is not the only classical method we can use. We also have Aristotle's analysis of any object in order to understand its nature. His power to observe is helpful for analysis of any object! Welcome to Aristotle's Four Causes!

"When dealing with people, remember you are not
dealing with creatures of logic, but with creatures bristling
with prejudice and motivated by pride and vanity."

—DALE CARNEGIE

The Power of Observation: Think like Aristotle!

Aristotle (384-322 BC), one of the most important philosophers ever in western thought and culture, sought to understand the nature of any object by evaluating its Four Causes, namely, its Material, Efficient, Formal, and Final Causes.

For example, let us consider Michelangelo's statue of David in Florence, Italy (1501-1504):

1   **Material Cause:** What is its composition? (e.g., single block of marble)

2   **Efficient Cause:** Who made it? What tools were used? What knowledge did he possess to make it? (e.g., Michelangelo between 1501-1504). Efficient cause is the ability for which it was created.

3   **Formal Cause:** What is it to be? (e.g., King David). It's essence, form, or function of a thing.

4   **Final Cause:** What is it for? (It commemorates biblical story of David preparing to fight Goliath in the Roman tradition). Final cause deals with the ultimate purpose of the object.

Socrates' Socratic Method and Aristotle's analysis of the nature of any object by seeking to discover its Four Causes, are complemented by the subsequent sevenfold criteria for evaluating truth-claims and worldview thinking!

Sevenfold Approach for Evaluating Truth-Claims and Worldview Thinking[11]

Why should we use this sevenfold method for evaluating truth-claims when taking someone's truth-claims and worldviews seriously? Consider the following reasons.

First, not all explanations are created equal. For example, many reasons and a number of explanations could be given for why my coffee mug is missing. I could have left the coffee mug in my sports car. Bob says I could have left my coffee mug at the lectern. Cynthia claims that the Greek god Pan is playing a playful prank on me. Don insists that I never brought a coffee cup to the university; it was a projection from my desires within. It could be that the university president wanted to show potential donors how impoverished their faculty members were; more money is needed and the state of this coffee mug shows them why! Therefore, while all these truth-claims may be earnestly made from wonderful people, not all of them are equal. No, what happened was that I accidentally left my coffee mug in my vehicle.

Second, we tend to rush to judgment without careful evaluation due to personal vices (bad habits) like impatience. We just want to move onto the next thing.

Third, we travel habituated paths of observation and interpretation. We have a tendency to think, feel, desire, and act in habituation. Therefore, this sevenfold method helps break us of rutted roads of analysis.

Fourth, we fail to be sharp, reasonable, and thorough in our evaluations because of other competing interests like our emotions, irrational impulses, longings, mesmerizing personalities, and self-interests.

Fifth, we use this sevenfold method because a truth-claim or even a worldview might pass a criterion but still not be the best explanation. For

---

[11] Adapted and expanded the criteria offered by William H. Halverson, *A Concise Introduction to Philosophy*, 383-409.

example, a truth-claim may be logical but lack evidences. Therefore, we need to examine truth-claims like a multifaceted diamond.

Sixth, mistakes can be costly and extract the best parts from us. If we rush to judgment, we might find ourselves in places we never thought we would go. Since ideas have consequences, it is possible that some evaluations may result in mistakes that could cost us a grade, a career, or loss of what we hold dear.

Seventh, we don't want to be misled or mislead others. We believe that thinking with excellence will consider how we might commit ourselves to the true good of others.

Eighth, we don't want to embrace something that will unnecessarily harm ourselves, others in our spheres of influence, and even our legacy.

Lastly, if we are not careful, then we could commit the fallacy of reductionism (also known as the analytic fallacy). The fallacy of reductionism occurs when we study the nature of something without examining its other related areas. Though the topic is discussed later in this chapter, the fallacy of reductionism is the neglect of context, a reducing down of something, ignoring inherent or dynamic relationships (e.g., origins; usage; interplays). This fallacy also finds expression when we universalize a theme or give it unlimited applications over and against its historical backdrop, purposes, or situational setting. For example, if one wants to study the nature of the flower and considers the roots, stem, leaves, and petals without examining how the water, sunlight, soil, and bees interact with the flower, one will have committed the fallacy of reductionism. Thus, when we divorce analysis from context we are likely to commit the fallacy of reductionism.

Likening this sevenfold approach to a multifaceted diamond whereby we examine a truth-claim or a worldview from different angles, this combinationalism test can be used to evaluate any truth-claim or worldview:

The following sevenfold approach assumes that (1) facts exist independently of our own thoughts; (2) we can identify things as they actually are; (3) our beliefs can match up or harmonize with things as they actually are, going beyond mere assumptions or opinions (which may be true or false).[12] In other words, we are affirming that truth corresponds with reality as it actually is, can identify things as they actually are, never fail, diminish, and change or be extinguished, and must be logical (e.g., adheres to law of non-contradiction). Peter McInerney puts it this way, "Truth is the accuracy of an account of the world. Beliefs are false when they depict things inaccurately, that is, when they portray facts that do not exist as existing."[13] Thus, from this understanding of what truth actually is, we evaluate truth-claims and worldviews and carefully examine them to determine if these truth-claims correspond with real facts. In other words, coupled with a correspondence view of reality, the following sevenfold approach or criteria helps us recognize or sort out what is actually true from that which is false:

1   **Logically Coherent:** The truth-claim or worldview must be free of logical inconsistencies (e.g., law of non-contradiction). Moreover, the truth-claim must harmonize (coherence) with what we already know to be true.

---

12   Peter K. McInerney, *Introduction to Philosophy* (New York: HarperCollins, 1992), 39.
13   Idem.

2 **Empirical Adequacy:** The truth-claim or worldview must have evidential value. Show me the evidences! Give me the physical data! Another way of looking at empirical adequacy is its physical testability.

But empirical testability can even be historical whereby we draw upon apparent memories, testimony of others; oral or written (e.g., eyewitnesses; primary documents; secondary documents; physical traces left behind that point to the event, person, or place discovered by disciplines like archeology; application of certain scientific principles and critical interactions). Just because we didn't see something occur in the past doesn't mean we don't have a sensible, reasonable, and empirically rooted criteria to determine what has actually happened.

"Don't believe everything you hear.
Real eyes realize real lies."

—TUPAC SHAKUR

3 **Existentially Relevant:** The truth-claim or worldview must be pertinent, germane, and relatable. In other words, this truth-claim must have an important relevance on the matter at hand.

4 **Workability:** If something is true, then it will work. How does this truth-claim or worldview "cash" out in real, beneficial ways? But if something works, it doesn't necessarily make it true (e.g., "con-artists"). But if true, then it will generate practical benefits or results.

5 **Viability:** The truth-claim or worldview must be able to be lived out. This test clarifies values, pursuits, and plans.

6 **Explanatory Power:** Does this truth-claim or worldview possess explanatory power in the area of comprehensiveness? Does it offer an explanation that is weighty, substantive whereby it pulls all things together? Does it shed light on other inquiries, insights, or discoveries?

7 **Ethical and Aesthetic Excellence:** Does this truth-claim or worldview possess moral and aesthetic qualities, virtues, duties, and

accountability that meaningfully improve or degrade what is good, honorable, true, trustworthy, and beautiful? Does it generate virtue or vice, contribute or degenerate one's wellbeing and the good of the community? Does it satisfy, conform to, and enrich our conscience or is it counter-intuitive, corrupting if not extracting the best parts of our personhood and even our community?

All three tools, namely, Socratic Method, Aristotle's Four Causes, and the sevenfold approach, presuppose, once again, that we live in an actual world and that reality corresponds to how things actually are. Thus, underpinning the investigations of truth-claims and worldviews we should ask (a) how the answers fit into the way things actually are (reality) and (b) how historically and scientifically testable the truth-claims are; can they be validated? In other words, what justification or sufficient reasons do we have to accept this truth-claim as knowledge (not mere personal belief)? Justification gives us the basis to know why a certain truth-claim is true.

"The most pervasive fallacy of philosophical thinking goes back to neglect of context."

—JOHN DEWEY

While these three types of tools are beneficial in thinking with excellence, it behooves us to be concerned with one of the most important fallacies we repeatedly observe in any analysis, critique, or investigation, namely, the fallacy of reductionism. This is where we now direct our attention.

The Felon of Fallacies! The Fallacy of Reductionism[14]

As stated earlier, the fallacy of reductionism occurs when we study the nature of something without examining its other related areas. The fallacy

---

[14]   Gregory F. Pappas, *John Dewey's Ethics: Democracy as Experience* (Bloomington: Indiana University Press, 2008), 26-28.

of reductionism is the neglect of context, a reducing down of something or ignoring something that is related to the object being studied. For example, we commit this fallacy when the results of a particular analysis are interpreted as complete in themselves apart from any context or other features. For example, humans are nothing more than biochemical machines; we are merely dancing to our DNA.

We commit this fallacy when we ignore context, elevate our conclusions, and give them unlimited applications (we universalize x without contextual sensitivity). For example, my marriage is a disappointment. Thus, all marriages are a disappointment.

Lastly, we commit the fallacy when we are selective in our emphasis apart from all related features. For example, when we only consider technical excellence in an art piece apart from historical context, intended meaning, thematic veracity, and the authenticity of the statement in the art-form by the artist, then we commit the fallacy of reductionism (see Chapter 11, "Analyze the Arts").

Keepin' It Real!

As you analyze other people's worldviews you will repeatedly discover, perhaps daily, four related problems: (1) arbitrary, prejudicial conjecture, (2) pre-commitments, (3) assumptions unacknowledged, and the (4) real possibility of self-deception. Let's further explore these four common occurrences.

The Problem of Arbitrary, Prejudicial Conjecture. As you analyze other people's worldviews, you will quickly observe common, random statements of conjecture in communications and conversations, conferences and conventions, the arts and the sciences. Often tainted by prejudice (e.g., anti-intellectual; philosophical; racial; religious; social), conjectures are assumptions made without proof. Their statements and proclamations are not researched, properly reasoned, or evidentially supported. When connected with other biased inferences, they reveal logical inconsistencies. Arbitrary, unsupported, and logically inconsistent truth-claims can become roadblocks to honest inquiry, rational discourse, the practice of civility, and even a better future. How? First, they lack rationality. Second, they frequently use emotionally charged (emotive) words that inflame tension and hinder honest dialogue. Lastly, they foster resentment in interpersonal relationships and the organized life of the community. Being unreasonable engenders unnecessary politics, fosters impoliteness, and stagnates progress. Moreover, arbitrariness is a fickle friend. Repeatedly ask these types of questions, "What's your basis for saying that?" If one can't defend a truth-claim, then it is likely conjecture.

The Problem of Pre-Commitments. While arbitrary, prejudicial conjecture is commonplace in every sphere of life, often flowing from our emotions or ideas we find attractive, we also have the pernicious and perennial problem of pre-commitments (as discussed in chapter three). Stronger than conjecture, they are commitments made to certain positions without substantiation. But like conjecture, they lack honest inquiry and research, evidence, and proper reasoning. In essence, pre-commitments are unsubstantiated allegiances apart from serious, careful investigations, rational thinking and empirical evidence. Pre-commitments can be dishonest positions for information is willfully ignored; it disagrees with what we want to believe. In other words, it is only affirming, agreeing, or advancing what we already embrace. While certain pre-commitments may later be proven to have sound justification, we often don't take the time to know if they do and to what extent. Pre-commitments can blind us terribly to openness and the pursuit of truth. Thus, we consistently need to examine one's pre-commitments. Why? History is the outworking of ideas in the lives of people, for better or for worse. But if we want to think with excellence, then we must go beyond our pre-commitments and be as honest as we can about our conversations, inquiries, objectives, processes, and conclusions. Consistently ask yourself and others, "What is your justification for embracing this position?"

> "I tore myself away from the safe comfort of certainties
> through my love for truth - and truth rewarded me."
>
> —SIMONE DE BEAUVOIR

The Problem of Assumptions. It is critical we understand the assumptions used, embraced, and proclaimed in any given community, context, or conversation. We must not take it for granted that we know the meaning of words, propositional statements, or beliefs in any situational setting, location, or activity (e.g., academic major; online educational classroom; work). Here's why. If we are rightfully aware of those shared assumptions, then there will be less opportunity for miscommunication and misunderstanding. Thus, know your people. Apprehend the assumptions discussed in any given communication, location, or practice. Ask good, clarifying questions. For example, "When you use that term, what do you mean?" "How are you using that word?" "How did you come to that conclusion?" Be sure to listen for the answer.

The Problem of Self-Deception. Critical thinking is incomplete until self-assumptions are analyzed. Don't merely examine a person's worldview or particular context without reflecting upon and testing your assumptions, what they are, and how they affect your observations, interpretations, and conclusions. In other words, consistently examine whether you have embraced arbitrary, prejudicial truth-claims. Test those assumptions by examining their (1) justification, (2) how they logically cohere with one another, and (3) express accurately the way things actually are. If you fail to do so, then you might find yourself rightly identified as "self-deceived."

"Self-deception" not only brings about conclusions that are inaccurate, non-beneficial, and tragic, but they also breed "other deceptions" as people embrace what you say without ever analyzing those truth-claims for themselves. Therefore, we not only owe it to ourselves to evaluate self-assumptions and truth-claims we make, but we are also encouraged to safeguard others from our own arbitrary, prejudicial assumptions. Consequently, wisdom finds expression, civility is cultivated, and social responsibility is upheld.

Therefore, in every analysis, look for three things:

1   Arbitrary, prejudicial conjecture;
2   Pre-commitments to a particular philosophical position without any substantial justification;
3   Lack of coherence between two or more truth-claims.

If we will integrate these insights into any analysis, whether our own or in the truth-claims made by others, then we will be on the road to thinking with excellence.

Conclusion

While everyone has beliefs, not all beliefs are valid. While everyone makes truth-claims, not all truth-claims are equal. While everyone has a worldview, not all worldviews possess the same strength. Some worldviews are actually very weak because they possess significant contradictions, logical inconsistencies, and lack of evidences. Therefore, in order to be the hero the world needs, follow the five:

Follow the Five:

1   When you encounter a truth-claim, a personal belief, or a different worldview, consistently ask (a) "What do you mean by _____?" and (b) "How did you come to that conclusion?"

2   Be the Socrates our society needs by being a good listener, asking good questions, and practicing civility (be respectful, polite, and non-irrational); follow the Socratic Method.

3   Investigate the nature of things like Aristotle did by evaluating their material, efficient, formal, and final causes.

4   To sort out what truth-claims, personal beliefs, or worldviews are actually true ("true truths"), use the sevenfold approach. Never simply assume what one states to be true. Inquire. Investigate. Analyze. Always resist rushing to a conclusion or judgment till truth-claims, personal beliefs, or worldviews are thoughtfully examined.

5   Never isolate an argument from its context less you commit the fallacy of reductionism. Think with excellence!

> "That's what we're missing. We're missing argument.
> We're missing debate. We're missing colloquy.
> We're missing all sorts of things. Instead, we're accepting."
>
> —Studs Terkel

LIFESAVING TIPS

"How Can I Have More Friends?"

Here are twelve maxims for interpersonal social skills you should consider on the first day of college or university experience & beyond:

1 Ask good questions. Know people's stories, what they like and dislike, who they are and what they do; Keep the focus on them!

2 Make eye contact, listen thoughtfully, and don't invade personal space. Grrrr!

3 Summarize, summarize, and summarize your responses! Please, we beg you!

4 Don't confuse someone's curiosity about what you enjoy to mean they want to do it too. Let their passions be their passions and don't judge them for it!

5 Ask yourself: How do others feel around you? Are they enriched or drained? Why?

6 Avoid redirecting conversations to yourself. Self-importance pushes people away from you. Personal admiration, entitlement, and an inflated ego are a "no-go." But also avoid excessive self-criticism.

7 Intellectually stretch yourself broadly and deeply. Study the arts and the humanities. It will do you good; it will round you out.

8 If given the opportunity, be adventurous. Travel. See how others live.

9 Consistently commit your will to the true good of others. Be a true friend!

10 Be a person of moral integrity. Maintain promises. Let your yes be yes and no be no. Avoid gossip. Be the change you want to see in others.

11   Be about truth and love in every dimension in life; both are inseparable. If you develop these traits as a way of living, then you will be attractive to others in the most beneficial ways.

12   Show sincere and thoughtful appreciation for what others do you for you. Gratitude is key!

"Everyone thinks of changing the world,
but no one thinks of changing himself."

—LEO TOLSTOY

CHAPTER FIVE

Five Ways of Seeing

"Successful problem solving requires finding the right solution to the right problem. We fail more often because we solve the wrong problem than because we get the wrong solution to the right problem."

—Russell L. Ackoff

O ne of the most valuable ways of thinking with excellence is to pursue a holistic approach of critical thinking. Like considering a vehicle to purchase, you want to carefully consider its individual parts, how it works as a whole, how it functions in the context in which it will be embedded, and what ways will it truly be a meaningful purchase. Therefore, this holistic approach will offer a way to not only help you from following one method alone, but also enable you to make wise choices, offer thorough evaluations, and avoid premature and faulty judgments. In fact, if you are willing to master this holistic method of critical analysis, then you will not only make connections that would be otherwise missed, you will develop practical skills that will enable you to do the following for the rest of your life:

1   Greater ability to decide between options. While certain opportunities may appear to be the same, when you use this holistic approach, you will likely discover which option(s) is (are) best for you and others involved.

2   Avoid premature judgments. Here you will likely avoid certain pitfalls of making a costly mistake.

3   Intelligence will be improved as you see relationships others can see.

4   You will stand out among others because most people are great in one approach, but neglect other ways of seeing. Consequently, what they see will be deficient. But not you! You will think with excellence.

5   If you struggle with fear of making mistakes, then this holistic approach to critical thinking will help alleviate that concern in a tremendous way.

"Simple can be harder than complex: You have to work hard
to get your thinking clean to make it simple. But it's worth it in the end
because once you get there, you can move mountains."

—STEVE JOBS

Synthetic Way of Thinking

While attending Dallas Theological Seminary and the University of Texas-Dallas, I (Paul) learned how to see things fit together, how separate elements come together (harmonize), and how things work as a whole. In essence, my professors taught me how to think synthetically. From the biblical languages to thinking theologically, they equipped me with skills to see how various parts work together, the contextual and historical origins where ideas, meaning, and symbols emerge, how to identify multiple connections, and what significances are engendered from those shared relationships. At the University of Texas at Dallas, I saw the relationship between the origin and use of ideas and culture, creativity and community, and identity and becoming. From those two rigorous institutions I was greatly equipped with rich skills of synthetic thinking. But what I came to discover is that my synthetic skills were not only inadequate, they were also considered unnecessary. Here's what happened.

What Is Synthetic Thinking?

The synthetic approach to evaluation focuses on seeing how a system works together as a whole and relates to the greater context or situational setting in which it is embedded. The synthetic approach not only examines how the various combination of arguments, information, objects, thoughts, or systems work together as a whole, looking at behaviors, contributions, and functions to each other and other interrelationships (such as its greater context), but can also generate enormous creativity and benefits by considering new combinations, organizations, and relationships. Here you also check for harmony (coherence) between those parts and the practical consequences the system generates.

I (Paul) had just finished giving a presentation on sociological epistemology to my fellow students and professor in a graduate course in epistemology at Texas A&M University. It was a paper on two subjects I love, namely, how we know something to be true (epistemology) and the study of human social behavior (sociology). But after receiving encouraging words of affirmation from other graduate students of philosophy, my professor, in not so uncertain terms, asked if I would follow her to her office. Her disappointment with my work was clear. I was flabbergasted. I was confused. I was shocked. But what I came to discover about myself through her changed everything.

In contrast to the encouragement I received from other students, she thought my paper on sociological epistemology was terrible. She said my extensive use of footnotes was wrong-headed. Instead of using Turabian format (which I dearly loved), I was told I should have written in first person whereby I actually could analyze the arguments apart from their authorial background, historical context, and cultural relationships. The emphasis was to be explicitly on the actual argument itself and counter-arguments. Each premise was to be broken down with utmost clarity, precision, and thoroughness. Coherence was to be applied to the argument. Revisions and rebuttals were to be given with the same force of clarity, correctness, and completeness.

Analytic Way of Thinking

What Is Analytical Thinking?

Analytical thinking is a step-by-step analysis whereby you scrutinize, dissect, and break down arguments, information, objects, thoughts, or systems into its various simpler, fundamental components, identifying their different categories or parts. You not only focus on facts, data and evidences, but you also eliminate unimportant or unnecessary information. Your reasoning process will be logical and harmonistic (coherence).

I was actually surprised by my professor's claim that she was not interested in historical context, syntheses, and other viewpoints. She only wanted my analysis, my understanding and critique of the author's central arguments, breaking it down into its various proponents. What she did not know (and what I did not tell her) is that I actually contacted the author and we had a rich dialogue about sociological epistemology the weekend before. But even if I had given her that information, she would have been more interested in breaking down the argument rather than learning about the historical and contextual relationship or insights shared between me and the author.

So, the initial words of affirmation from my fellow students quickly dissipated with feelings of embarrassment, insecurity, and failure. In fact, given my prior accolades and successes at the other graduate institutions I attended, those weighty feelings were long standing. But what I could not do is give up! Interestingly, what happened that day in her office actually put me on a new path. My failure, which was actually rooted in non-willful ignorance, was translated into a set of thinking skills I use today.

After "beating myself up" for a while, I purchased a book, which she recommended, and which I continue to recommend for those interested in improving one's grammar, clarity, and structure in argumentation, namely, A. P. Martinich's *Philosophical Writing*. Another book that will supplement one's writing is *Woe Is I: The Grammarphobe's Guide to Better English in Plain English* by Patricia T. O'Conner.[15]

> "The goal of analysis, in its broad sense, is to make philosophy less difficult than it otherwise would be. This is just a corollary of a more general principle: anyone can make a subject difficult; it takes an accomplished thinker to make a subject simple."[16]
>
> —A.P. MARTINICH

But the story does not end there. A couple of years later I was privileged to hear Dr. J. P. Moreland, a very respected author and philosopher who not only received a graduate degree from Dallas Theological Seminary, but also a Ph.D. in philosophy from the University of Southern California. Since

---

[15] See Patricia T. O'Conner, *Woe Is I: The Grammarphobe's Guide to Better English in Plain English*, 4th ed. (New York: Riverside Books, 2019).

[16] A. P. Martinich, *Philosophical Writing: An Introduction*: 4th ed. (Malden, MA: John Wiley and Sons, 2016), 18.

we both studied under some of the same thinkers at Dallas Theological Seminary, I asked him if his experience was similar to mine, namely, being trained to think synthetically but later learning how to think analytically. While his experience is his alone to tell, I do remember his conclusion. He said something like, "Paul, it is rare to find philosophers and theologians who can do both. But if you can master both, synthetic and analytical thinking, then you will be able to do what few can."

Therefore, while I deeply appreciate the hard lessons learned, a kick in the pants, so to speak, for my failure to think analytically but synthetically, I will never devalue the skills of synthetic thinking. In fact, I look at both approaches as tools to engage any serious inquiry. You can, too!

Critical analysis also benefits from three other approaches, namely, lateral thinking, existential analysis, and practical analysis.

Lateral Way of Thinking[17]

Lateral thinking, created by Dr. Edward de Bono, is an alternative approach to analytic thinking. In essence, this type of approach assumes *creativity as a thinking skill*. Proponents of lateral thinking begin by asking creative questions in order to think about new possibilities, listen to alternative possibilities, and uncover what we might be failing to observe. Here are some questions asked by proponents of lateral thinkers:

1　What can be?

2　How can we think outside of the box?

3　How can we change the rules?

4　How can we think about this idea not following the traditional forms of logic?

5　What are we overlooking?

---

[17]　See Edward de Bono, *Lateral Thinking: Step by Step* (New York: Harper & Row, 1970); *Six Thinking Hats*, rev. & exp. (Mica Management Resources, Inc. 1999).

6   What are unusual perspectives we can use?

7   Can we arrange the argument, idea, or problem, in ways foreign to our
     normal way of evaluating things?

Lateral creative thinking breaks away from habituated paths, rutted roads,
and predictive patterns of thinking. This approach is framed by possibilities, probabilities, and alternatives, resists premature judgments and static
routes, preserves openness, and involves multiple angles.

Moreover, the lateral, creative approach complements other ways of thinking such as giving us permission to consider our feelings, hunches, and
intuitions, what is different, foreign or novel, and put a pause on all the
reasons why something will not work following usual patterns of analyses.

"The biggest problem facing the world today
is not climate change at all, but inadequate thinking."

—EDWARD DE BONO

Existential Way of Thinking[18]

Critical, holistic analysis not only benefits from synthetic thinking, analytic
thinking, and lateral, creative thinking, but also from existential thinking.

How will this argument, idea, position, or system be relevant to our personhood, our identity, our meaning, and our becoming? How will they
contribute to our significance, our hopes, our dreams, and our destinies?
Will our identity, meaning, purpose, and significance be marginalized or
enriched? In what ways does this argument, idea, position, or system relate
to our existence, the shaping of our personhood, and our moral stance in
this world, each other, and God? Does this idea displace or help? Does it

---

[18]   See Peter Kreeft, *Christianity for Modern Pagans: Pascal's Pensées* (San
       Francisco: Ignatius Press, 1993); Thomas E. Wartenberg, *Existentialism: A
       Beginner's Guide* (Oxford, UK: Oneworld, 2008).

realize our humanity? Or does it marginalize or enrich our lives given the deep struggles of our human condition?

> "People fall so in love with their pain, they can't leave it behind.
> The same as the stories they tell. We trap ourselves."
>
> —CHUCK PALAHNIUK

Practical Way of Thinking

At this level we pursue our inquiry on the prescriptive level. We begin by examining "ought" claims. These "ought" claims are application and can deal with rules, commands, traditions, precepts, and principles in many spheres of authority: cultural, familial, political, religious, social, and theological.

Here we can also consider case studies. What happened when those arguments, ideas, positions, and systems were followed? What were the short-term and long-term consequences? How were lives affected?

Conclusion

If you can apply this holistic approach to any investigation, then you will not only be thinking critically, you will also be thinking with excellence! Take any argument (e.g., climate change; kalam cosmological argument for God's existence), idea (e.g., racism; natural, moral law), position (e.g., new atheism; homeschool versus public school) or system (e.g., socialism; dispensationalism) and apply the following five steps:

> "I am always doing that which I cannot do,
> in order that I may learn how to do it."
>
> —PABLO PICASSO

Five Ways of Seeing: Holistic Approach to Critical Analysis

STEP 1
Analytic

Dissect argument, eliminate non-essentials, & focus on the premises of the argument. A logically valid argument depends upon the truthfulness of the premises. If the premises are true, then the conclusion will be true as well.

STEP 2
Synthetic

Look at the argument, idea, position, or system as a whole for harmony, internal consistency, & logical integrity. See how all things relate to one another & function as a whole. Also, consider its historical & situational context, origins, & use.

STEP 3
Practical

Problem-solving on a prescriptive level. What commands, principles, or "ought" claims are advocated from this argument, idea, position, or system-whether cultural, familial, political, religious, social, or theological? What are the possible immediate & long-term consequences? How will it affect the formation of your character, well-being, community, & the true good of others? Also, look at case studies. If this argument, idea, position, or system has already been considered & actualized, then what does history record? History is the outworking of ideas in society.

STEP 4
Existential

How will this argument, idea, position, or system relate to the deep existential struggles of your human condition: aspirations, development, fulfillment, happiness, identity, legacy, meaning, purpose, significance, & wholeness?

STEP 5
Lateral

Using creativity as a thinking skill, think outside of the box; suspend routine types of analyses. Unusual approaches can be considered. Feelings, hunches, & intuition are acceptable for consideration. Be creative in your analysis; what are you still overlooking? What are you missing?

Consequently, you will gain an incredible clarity, outpace others, and contribute to a particular problem in a way others will be unable to do. Coupled with personal integrity whereby your "yes" is yes and "no" is no, promises are fulfilled, and honesty is your reputation, you will make your life count for something great. Moreover, you will experience a certain satisfaction that is not generated by those who seek to only do what is minimal, who remain too comfortable in their current state. Remember, your contributions can change the lives of many! But be warned! Do not commit the fallacy of reductionism by reducing your inquiry only to one approach to the neglect of all other approaches. Use the five-fold approach in any serious investigation! You may not only make new discoveries, but you might also become tomorrow's hero our world needs today!

> "The essence of the independent mind lies not in
> what it thinks, but in how it thinks."
>
> —CHRISTOPHER HITCHENS

LIFESAVING TIPS

"How Can I Make My Life Count for Something Great?"

1   Proactively strive to be a person of intellectual and moral excellence.

2   Know what you believe and why. Build a worldview that possesses the greatest structural integrity.

3   Be a person of integrity. Let your yes be yes and no be no; fulfill your promises.

4   Commit your will to the true good of others.

5   Enable others unto success. When they succeed, you succeed.

6   Be zealous about the good things of life (e.g., what is inherently good, true, and beautiful).

7   Instead of immobilizing yourself, use your anxiety, failures, mistakes, past, and problems to propel you towards excellence.

8   Enjoy activities, things, and rich experiences, but live for what matters most.

9   Anticipate, meet, and exceed the practical needs of others.

10   Develop your imagination.

11   Understand the perspectives of others. Be a good listener; ask good questions to understand; talk less.

12   Repeat 1-11 in the moment-by-moment decisions you make in daily living.

"Never forget that only dead fish swim with the stream."

—MALCOLM MUGGERIDGE

"There Is Just Something Not Right! I Feel like I Am Lost, Living in a Dream?"

Are you anxious? Depressed? Lethargic? Gaining weight? Poor attention span? Are you having trouble knowing what is real? Things are not making sense to you? You feel like you are "living in a dream?" Loss of creativity and wonder in the way you are experiencing life? Has life become obscure?

Given our digital age and the rapid changes of technology, many of us, whether young or old, are spending more time inside than outside. Consequently, our constant "connection" to technology is creating a "disconnection" with physical nature. Coupled with an overstimulation of our senses, online capabilities involving work, play, social life, and studies, and our range of vision limited to our indoor abodes, many of us are struggling with what is described by Richard Louv as "Nature Deficit Disorder" (NDD) from his 2008 work, *Last Child in the Woods: Saving Our Children From Nature-Deficit Disorder.*[19]

While not a clinical, medical, or psychological term, NDD is symptomatic of not "plugging into" nature. We are among the first-generation in human history whose occupation, play, studies, relationships, and vocations can all take place indoors with technology at our fingertips, needs and desires speedily if not immediately met, and the comforts indoor living often possesses. In contrast, people in the past worked outside with their hands, plowed the land, hunted for their food, and played in the open air; they did not have the powers that flow from a touch of a button or a voice command. This digital sphere of living is our new habitation - with all of its pleasures, possibilities, promises, and perils.

"In every walk with nature one receives far more than he seeks."

—John Muir

---

[19]   See Richard Louv, *Last Child in the Woods: Saving Our Children From Nature-Deficit Disorder* (Chapel Hill, NC: Algonquin Books of Chapel Hills, 2005, 2008).

Therefore, if things are not making sense to you, you feel overwhelmed, or you feel like you need a break, regularly spend some time outside. Nature is not only worth beholding on its own terms, but it can also be therapeutic to your whole person. In fact, one of the benefits of consistently, diligently, and respectfully taking time to walk in a park, sit outside and observe the physical nature that surrounds you in a bit of "green space," or look across upon the horizon, up into the starry sky, or down upon a nearby pond or stream, is that your ability to think with excellence will improve. Nature can have a calming effect against all the confinements, controls, and computers. Noise is exchanged for silence, a pause, "a breather." Silence is a respite from all the business, demands, and constantly moving images. We can find expression when we step outside, feel the sunlight touch our skin, feel the breeze move through our hair, and hear the sounds of nature (e.g., the birds sing).

Consistent exposure to nature benefits us holistically, offering a type of re-calibration we all need or even some type of catharsis, a release from emotional weightiness, painful tensions, and heavy woes, even if for a moment. Physical nature can help bring us "back to reality."

By regularly adding a "social media cleanse" as a recurring practice, we are likely to gain greater clarity about what is valuable, improve conversational skills, and recapture some of the aesthetic experiences and wondrous moments that are occurring all around us. Moreover, the forces of nature can clarify our values. But just putting the smartphone down or turning away from the laptop, and looking a person in the eye, can instill respect of you from people you encounter, whether colleagues, family, friends, and strangers. Why? Doing so gives them attention, it shows them worth; it gives them a proper hearing. It demonstrates that you are taking the time to look them in the eyes and listen; non-verbal language alone offers significance.

My (Paul) own daughter, Julianna Grace, and her best friend, Sierra Lynn, are taking the entire break between fall and spring semesters to "cleanse" themselves from social media. I asked, "Why?" She said to "recapture clarity, have better focus." Likewise, don't let technology marginalize your humanity, shape you in ways you will later regret, diminish the values of interpersonal friendships and social etiquette, or control you whereby you are being monitored, governed, and ruled by technology. Stated differently, don't allow technology to manage you; you manage technology.

I (Raul) always make sure that my four children (Colin, Stefan, Aiden, and Elena) take breaks from their video games, phones, and TVs. I call them "health breaks." In response, they often ask what they should do instead. I tell them to go outside and they sometimes laugh, think I'm joking, or roll their eyes. You see, we live in the country. I want them to appreciate the outdoors. And while I do think that they do, indeed, appreciate it, they oftentimes forget how wonderful it can be. Still, I get asked on a regular basis by my kids, "What do I do outside?" I tell them "breathe the air," "smell the flowers," "look at the sky," "sit and read or write under a tree," "lay in a hammock," "play football." The last activity is often a family affair. I enjoy throwing the football with my kids. We also play basketball and participate in ring toss and beanbag toss. After a while, my kids forget about their devices. They can be seen laughing and enjoying their time. Their stress levels appear to diminish, and mine does as a result as well!

In a nutshell (from a tree outside), detaching ourselves from technology and attaching ourselves to physical nature on a *consistent basis* is critical. This change of activity not only helped both of our families, but it qualitatively nourished us, connecting us to our past, widening our understanding of the world, improving our abilities to relate to one another, and promoting thinking with excellence in a way that cultivates a certain type of cognitive and existential freedom and wholeness.

"There are moments when all anxiety and stated toil
are becalmed in the infinite leisure and repose of nature."

—HENRY DAVID THOREAU

CHAPTER SIX

Tips for Truth

"The less time you spend with Truth, the easier it is to believe lies."

—Lecrae

O ne evening I (Paul) was speaking before a group of eighty people at a college in East Texas about the rise and decline of our western culture. I was a senior at the university. As soon as I began to speak, I recognized this rather big fella sitting among the gathering. I was immediately intimidated. It was not his weight that I feared; it was his reputation. He was notorious in our community for serving as a bit of a "gadfly." Like Socrates, he questioned others who did not share his naturalistic, evolutionary view of reality. Sure enough, when it came to question/answer time, he immediately raised his hand. Intimated by his presence, I was hoping for the best. But fortunately for me, he asked, "You used the word 'truth' quite a bit for tonight. Could you define it for me?" Using the Socratic Method, I realized he had me. My response was rather poor. See, I repeatedly used a word that I couldn't define. I am all the more grateful for that event because it taught me a valuable lesson, namely, anytime you emphasize or repeat a significant word like truth, you better be prepared to define it! Indeed, what is truth? Why even think about truth? Consider the following insights from philosopher Douglas Groothuis:

"The word truth is a staple in every language. We cannot imagine a human language lacking the concept of truth. Such a language would never inform anyone of anything; it would lack any intellectual access to reality. No language *qua* [as] language could be so constrained (although some political and celebrity 'discourse' come close). The idea of truth is part of the intellectual oxygen we breathe. Whenever we state an opinion, defend or critique an argument, ask a question, or investigate one kind of assertions or another, we presuppose the concept of truth-even if we don't directly state the word, even if we deny that truth is real or knowable. The notion of truth haunts us, ferreting out our shabby thinking, our lame excuses, our willful ignorance and our unfair attacks on the views of others, both the living and the dead. Conversely, when our own ideas are misrepresented or our personal character falsely maligned, we object by appealing to something firm that should settle the issue-namely, the truth. Truth seems to stand over like a silent referee, arms folded confidently, ears open, eyes staring intently and authoritatively into everything and missing nothing. Even when an important truth seems out of reach on vital matters, we yearn for it as we yearn for a long-lost friend or the parent we never knew. Yet when the truth unmasks and convicts us, and refuse to return its gaze, we seek to banish it in favor of our own self-serving and protective version of reality."[20]

Truth-Claims in Triage

We came to discover in chapter four, "Be the Hero the World Needs: Analyze Truth-Claims," that in order to think with excellence we must evaluate truth-claims. Why? Every day we are being bombarded with truth-claims. From images we see, the celebrities we admire, teachers we trust, and parents we love, the news sources we watch and listen, and the politicians we hear, we are constantly being exposed to a barrage of contradictory truth-claims. But to sort out what really is factual and what is conjecture, we must be like a crime investigator and sort out what is true from what is not. Though

---

[20] Douglas Groothuis, *Christian Apologetics* (Grand Rapids: IVP Academic, 2011), 139.

we use the sevenfold criteria for evaluating truth-claims (given in chapter four), we need to take a closer look at three major approaches used by those who take truth-claims and personal beliefs seriously. Consider the following three major approaches for coming to know what is true: (1) Correspondence Views; (2) Coherence Views; (3) Pragmatic Views.

> "Truth is so obscure in these times, and falsehood so established, that, unless we love the truth, we cannot know it."
>
> —BLAISE PASCAL

Correspondence View of Truth[21]

The correspondence view of truth states that the truth-claim made by someone will be true if and only if it corresponds with reality as it is. In other words, the truth-claim will match up to how things actually are; what is true will be faithful to reality. Aristotle is famous for advocating this view and it is the dominant view in Western thought and culture about how we know something to be true, in part, because it appeals to common sense; this is how we live in other practical dimensions of life (e.g., driving vehicles; folding clothes; making meals). Often times called "realism," this view champions the following presuppositions:

1   Truth is that which corresponds to reality.

2   Truth is telling it like it is.

3   Truth identifies things as they actually are.

4   Truth can never fail, diminish, change, or be extinguished. So, whether one recognizes what is true or not, it stands true nonetheless. Truth is not dependent on personal perspective because we exist in a "real" world. Stated differently, reality confers what is true and what is not; we do not. Rather, we submit to reality as it actually is (even if we don't like it).[22]

---

[21]   McInerney, *Introduction to Philosophy*, 39.

[22]   Mortimer J. Adler, *Aristotle for Everybody* (New York: Simon & Schuster, 1978).

The correspondence view of truth is valued throughout history for it is deemed common sense and practical in every area of life. Factual communication, learning, and knowing how to do something accurately, demands a correspondence view of truth. Your studies, in part, are an attempt to understand what is factually true. Curiosity, creativity, innovation, and scientific advancement and discoveries, a matching of ideas to what is factual, are born from our ability to know reality (e.g., landing on the moon; medicine to fight diseases; caring for our environment). While some of us may wish for an alternative reality (e.g., Tolkien's Middle Earth; Marvel's Universe), reality is what it is. But flowing from this correspondence view of truth we can look and explore the universe with wonder, understand ourselves, probe our deepest mysteries, and cultivate resources for a better future. In sum, truth is found in correspondence.

To deny the correspondence view of truth for other views is an attempt to use correspondence (it is self-defeating). If truth-claims are not able to match up with reality, then it is impossible to know what is true or false, correct or incorrect, authentic or inauthentic, whether abstract or concrete.

The correspondence view is anti-reductionistic since the object (referent) can be physical or abstract. Abstract realities would include mathematical truths and ideas (e.g., the ideas in your own mind). Even moral statements (e.g., "Lying is wrong") are true if they accurately match up with reality.

"Whoever is careless with the truth in small matters
cannot be trusted with important matters."

—Albert Einstein

139-142; McInerney, *Introduction to Philosophy*, 39.

Thus, a truth-claim is not true because of authority positions, mesmerizing personalities, or powerful personal feelings. Instead, according to this view, facts determine what is true. A truth-claim is not true because we believe it. Rather, we believe the truth-claim because it is true. While we are free to have our own opinions about a given matter, if something is true, then it is true regardless of what we think, believe, or feel, for truth is built upon facts, not mere opinions.

A truth-claim is given by someone.

Does the truth-claim correspond with reality as it actually is?

If so, then the truth-claim is true.

One of the most significant difficulties with correspondence theories of truth is how to account for moral statements such as "lying is wrong." How does one evaluate such a moral truth-claim according to a correspondence view of truth?

For the theist (that is, one who believes God is both infinite and personal) who embraces a correspondence view of truth, this is not a problem. Why? They contend moral statements are able to be tested against reality because, God who is the Creator and Sustainer of all of reality (both physical and spiritual), has disclosed objective moral laws for all to follow regardless of time, space, or culture. In particular, they presuppose God Himself as the foundation for evaluating moral duties and values. Thus, any moral truth-claim God discloses (e.g., natural, moral law; special revelation) will flow from Him who is the sum-total of His infinite perfections (e.g., goodness; justice). Only minds emit meaning.

For example, consider this philosophical argument from Cambridge philosopher W. E. Sorley (1855-1935):[23]

1   There is an objective moral law that is independent of human consciousness of it, and that exists in spite of human lack of conformity to it:

    a   Persons are conscious of such a law beyond themselves;

    b   Persons admit its validity is prior to their recognition of it;

    c   Persons acknowledge its claim on them, even while not yielding to it;

    d   No finite mind completely grasps its significance;

    e   All finite minds together have not reached complete agreement on its meaning, nor conformity with its ideal.

2   But ideas exist only in minds.

3   Therefore, there must be a supreme Mind (beyond all finite minds) in which this objective moral law exists.

Therefore, to make a claim that something is "evil" or "good" (e.g., genocide is evil; saving an orphanage from a fire is "good") or that the world is getting worse or better, implies a standard reference point, an ontological foundation that is absolute, objective, and universal.

> "What I like about experience is that it is such an honest thing.
> You may take any number of wrong turnings; but keep your eyes open
> and you will not be allowed to go very far before the warning signs
> appear. You may have deceived yourself, but experience is not trying to
> deceive you. The universe rings true wherever you fairly test it."
>
> —C. S. Lewis

---

[23]   Paul R. Shockley, "Philosophy of Religion: Arguments for God's Existence," *www.prshockley.org*. Retrieval Date: 6 September 2018.

Coherence View of Truth

Coherence theories of truth contend a belief or truth-claim is valid if it logically coheres or harmonizes with the rest of one's beliefs. The stronger the coherence, the more likely it is true. The key is logical consistency between truth-claims or beliefs. This approach is helpful if analyzing how beliefs harmonize with other beliefs, especially in evaluating worldviews, philosophical and religious paradigms, and theological systems:

Truth-Claims

Coherent set of beliefs

How do these truth-claims or beliefs harmonize with what you already know to be true?

The greater the coherence, the more likely the truth-claim being tested is true.

Coherence is like the relationship of jigsaw puzzle pieces.[24] The goal is to find the right pieces, assembling the most complete picture.

Now, these form a conception of the world, even though there is no independent world, and so are true. For example, the belief that your vehicle is running well seems to be true because it coheres with what you see, what you can touch, what you know about other engines, and many other things you believe.

"The discovery of truth is prevented more effectively,
not by the false appearance things present and which mislead
into error, not directly by weakness of the reasoning powers,
but by preconceived opinion, by prejudice."

—Arthur Schopenhauer

---

[24] McInerney, *Introduction to Philosophy*, 40.

One presupposition that undergirds coherence is the fact that we can't stand outside of our worldviews, comparing our assumptions with the world as it actually is. We are within culture and don't rise above it. Consequently, we take our beliefs (particular puzzle pieces) and see if they can fit together with other settled true beliefs into a broader picture of what we believe reality actually to be.

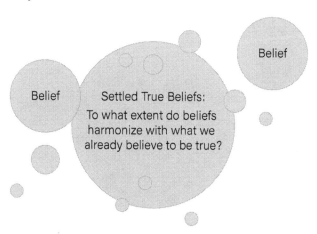

Yet, coherent view of truth presupposes that we don't have a direct awareness of reality. But does this philosophical assumption possess explanatory power in the way you live your life? For example, even right now you are able to recognize this text, *Thinking with Excellence*, for what it is; you have the capacity to identify and categorize. From many observations, you are able to develop a concept of what this text is. You are able to associate a term with your awareness of this book by use of senses, reasoning, and memory. *Thinking with excellence* is indeed that kind of thing, namely a text. You are able to re-observe and confirm what had already been seen.

One central problem with coherence views is that a set of statements may harmonize with each other but still fail to correspond with reality. While we consider the coherent approach to be helpful for thinking with excellence, it is insufficient if exclusively applied for knowing something to be true. Why? For example, you can have a set of beliefs that are not only logical but also can cohere or harmonize together yet do not match up with the way things really are. Notwithstanding, coherence is a necessary test for evaluating truth-claims, one's worldview, and various systems of thought. We believe coherence is a beneficial tool with the correspondence of reality as the foundation for assessing truth-claims.

Pragmatic View of Truth[25]

Pragmatic theories of truth contend that if truth-claims or beliefs lead to actions that have utility or bring beneficial results, they are considered true. In essence, pragmatists like Charles Sanders Peirce, William James, and John Dewey, embraced the view that truth is what works; truth is successful problem-solving.

Thus, we would consider beliefs to be true if using those beliefs allow us to accomplish our objectives in the world, generating beneficial results. In essence, we treat a truth-claim like the experimental method in science, that is, we test a hypothesis and evaluate its results, hoping for nutritious, qualitative, and positive outcomes. False beliefs are those that are ultimately not useful. Using false beliefs does not help us accomplish our objectives in the world. For example, the beliefs about magic elf-stones are false since they do not actually work in fighting evil. Therefore, each belief is evaluated on the basis of its usefulness.

One particular strength of a pragmatic theory of truth is its openness to experiment and not embrace a system of thought that is closed or static. Pragmatists will examine various philosophical ideas as "tools" to help achieve qualitatively beneficial results in the way we actually live, move, and have our becoming.

Yet, pragmatic theories of truth are questioned about how we determine what is "good," what does it mean for something to "work," and what are

---

[25] Ibid., 40-41. See David Hildebrand, *Dewey: A Beginner's Guide* (Oxford, UK: Oneworld, 2008); William James, *Pragmatism* (Cambridge, MA: Harvard University Press, 1907, 1978). Israel Scheffler, *Four Pragmatists: A Critical Introduction to Peirce, James, Mead, and Dewey* (London: Routledge, 1974); Paul R. Shockley, *Worship as Experience: An Inquiry into John Dewey's Aesthetics, The Community, and the Local Church* (Nacogdoches, TX: Stephen F. Austin State University Press, 2018), 16-52.

the causal connections between beliefs and results. But perhaps one of the most challenging difficulties is when we discover that a false belief engenders beneficial results. What are we to do?

Some beliefs may be false yet useful. Let's assume I believed I received an F for a course in my major. Consequently, I was so grieved because of the level of my investment in that course that I became emotionally despondent. I dropped out of the university my senior year and joined the military. I recovered from my grief as I found myself advancing very quickly in military rank; it has been a hand-in-glove sensation; military life fits who I am. But low and behold, I later received a certified letter stating that the university has been trying to reach me. Therefore, I needed to contact the registrar's office for them to know where they should mail my degree. It turns out that I didn't fail the course even though I believed I had failed. Thus, while the belief I failed the course was false, it generated a new direction in my life that produced very beneficial results that I would not have known otherwise.

Second, "a con-artist" may exploit others, generating lots of beneficial results, yet fail to truthfully represent what he or she claims to be. Thus, some things may work but do not correspond to the way things actually are.

While pragmatic theories of truth are understood in terms of experience, practice, results, or that which works, by themselves, they are insufficient. But when anchored to a correspondence view of truth and used alongside coherence view, they become powerful tools for evaluating truth-claims, beliefs, and worldviews.

To be sure, while these are the normative views of how one can know what is true, namely, correspondence, coherence, and pragmatic, we would be remiss not to mention an on-going 20th century movement known as continental philosophy. In some of your classes, correspondent, coherent, and pragmatic tests for knowing truth may be challenged, claiming truth is rooted in language, not reality. Welcome to Continental Philosophy!

Continental Theories of Knowing[26]

While its seminal ideas may be found in ancient thinkers like Protagoras (c. 485-415 BC), who claimed, "man is the measure of all things," several theories of truth arose in Continental Europe in the 20th-century known as Critical Theory, Structuralism, Postmodernism, and Post-Structuralism. Instead of presupposing reality as it is as the foundation, proponents contend that reality, truth, and values are determined, shaped, and empowered by social constructions. A social construct is an idea, belief, value, or practice that originated within and is accepted by a particular culture. Thus, these ideas or beliefs are not designed or discovered in reality as it is, or are divinely disclosed to us, but are created *within* culture. But these ideas or beliefs don't merely originate in culture; some of them have the power to shape society.

Some ideas, beliefs, and truth-claims are so persuasive that they are often misinterpreted as being "objective truths" by authorities, institutions, powerful personalities, and traditions. The masses, for the most part, believe these ideas to be true without ever questioning, challenging, or doing anything to evoke substantive change. But others revolt against certain social constructions hoping for change that is necessary for a better future. A few react for the love of anarchy and chaos. And then there are those who take action against social constructions to fulfill their own personal agendas and quest for personal gain. If one can repeat a truth-claim long enough and by enough authorities, institutions, personalities, and other mediums such as the arts (e.g., art; films; songs), then people will eventually assume that the truth-claim is actually true (this approach can lead people to commit logical fallacies like the bandwagon fallacy or novelty fallacy in logical thinking; see chapter 7). Examples of social constructions include class distinctions, dating practices, and racial segregation. Social constructions can benefit or degrade people's lives.

26 Brooke Noel Moore and Kenneth Bruder, *Philosophy: Power of Ideas*, 9th ed. (New York: McGraw-Hill, 2014), 11-13. See also Simon Critchley and William R. Schroader, eds., *A Companion to Continental Philosophy* (New York: Blackwell Publishers, 1998, 1999); Stephen H. Daniel, *Contemporary Continental Thought* (Upper Saddle, NJ: Prentice Hall, 2005); David West, *An Introduction to Continental Philosophy* (Cambridge, MA: Polity Press, 1996).

"The great enemy of the truth is very often not the lie,
deliberate, contrived and dishonest, but the myth,
persistent, persuasive and unrealistic."

—President John F. Kennedy

Why believe truth is a social construction and nothing more? Continental philosophers contend that truth is not based on logic, but rhetoric or language. Thus, continental philosophers seek to deconstruct language to see how linguistic expressions are used. They read and re-read looking for what is deeper, forgotten, marginalized, and overlooked in interpretations. Why are specific ideas suspiciously compelling? What is being stated and not stated? For them, all meaning is relative to a particular context, culture, or situation (conventionalism). Since all truth is conditioned by one's perspective (perspectivalism), continental thinkers not only argue that there is no one-to-one correspondence between words and the meanings they confer (referentialism), they also assert that one cannot ever exhaust all possible meanings (semantic progressivism). Therefore, they will argue for what may be termed as deconstructionism.

Deconstructionists not only challenge any over-arching, secure, universal, or ultimate meaning or what we call "meta-narratives," but seek to "deconstruct" the underlying presuppositions (fixed biases) and preunderstandings (moldable influences) that "infect" any and every interpretation, whether historical, literary, philosophical, political, or religious. Meta-narratives may even be perceived as alienating, oppressive, and exploitative. How they "deconstruct" is by not only arguing against fixed rules of analysis, but also seeking to expose, critique, resist, and displace binary assumptions, interpretations, aesthetic, moral, political, religious and social values and that arise in community and authority structures. They reject a "God-like viewpoint" for conclusions or judgments made are done *within* culture, not above or outside of culture. Deconstructionism is subversive, exposing "historical" interpretations and social complexities, constructions, and contradictions. Consequently, they will reconstruct meaning, looking for meaning beyond textual meaning or authorial intent. In fact, deconstructionism not only involves a dismantling of authorial meaning but also a reconstruction of meaning; the possibilities of other meanings are open-ended; meaning is always in a state of re-creation. In other words, language/meaning is always in flux. One of the most significant reasons why certain beliefs or ideas are long-held is because they are not only found to be compelling, but also because they become *ingrained* into what we think, how we think, the investigations we pursue, and the conclusions we make.

Continental philosophy is considered to be rivals to three other philosophical traditions, namely, analytic philosophy, American philosophy, and Thomistic philosophy.

Critical Theory: People, authority, and institutions can only be understood in the context of their assumptions, presuppositions, and practices. They critique their own ideals and practices.
Proponents: Theodor Adorno; Walter Benjamin; Eric Fromm; Max Horkheimer; Herbert Marcuse.

Structuralism: What are the conventions, principles, and rules that preside over language and social systems?
Proponents: Roman Jakobson; Claude Levi-Strauss; Jacques Lacan.

Postmodernism: Assuming that fixed meaning is not possible, what are the assumptions in language? Since meaning can only be found in experience, all words, definitions, and language are always in flux.
Proponents: Jacques Derrida; Francois Lyotard; Richard Rorty; Michel Foucault.

Post-Structuralism: What are the authorities, discourses, and linguistic social practices, processes, and perceptions that shape society, life and thought, what is real, true, and moral? Language, concepts, and experiences are intelligible, relatable, and compelling within relationships created, formed, and interwoven bodily, politically, and socially.
Proponents: Michael Foucault; Gilles Deleuze.

Perhaps one of the most interesting contributions of continental philosophy is from Michel Foucault (1926-1984), a French postmodernist and post-structuralist. Foucault offered a "forensic" type of historical, philosophical analysis whereby he criticized power structures in society, exploring the bilateral relationships between power, knowledge, and social control.[27] This was expressed in two methods: (1) Archaeological Method: archaeology (not to be confused with the field of archeology in uncovering history by examining what humans have physically created e.g., the City of David in Jerusalem; Pyramids in Egypt), is a method that examines our present situation, undermining the idea of advancement by exploring the micro-level structures of power in history; (2) Genealogical Method: entails the investigation of the structures that define the way we think about subjects such as madness, sexuality, and war.

These two types of analyses are helpful in the sense that it motivates us to investigate not only the answers given to truth-claims but also how the questions themselves are raised. What authorities, influences, and sources are used to frame the very questions and shape the responses given? For example, how are media, social utilities, celebrities, and institutional authorities framing, influencing, and molding the way we understand things?

Therefore, post-structuralism, like the other movements of continental philosophy, whether critical theory, structuralism, and postmodernism, is logically incoherent, lacks empirical adequacy and explanatory power, is riddled by fact/value splits, and ultimately is unworkable in daily living. Why? Continental philosophers locate "truth" (with a little "t"; no objective, over-arching, transcendent "T" for truth) in language and not logic (see chapter seven, "Lead with Logic").

However, there are benefits to their analyses that are worth considering by asking what forces are involved in attempting to shape our understanding of what is real, true, good, beautiful, and personally significant. We can even deceive ourselves into believing certain things to be true. Self-deception can be powerful. But reality, as it is, has a way of breaking through the personal beliefs we so desperately want to embrace and the "worlds" we attempt to create. When those moments occur, disillusionment, regret, and worldview fracturing find expression. But when honest inquiry harmonizes with things as

---

27 Paul R. Shockley, "A Way of Seeing War and Peace: The Methodologies of Michel Foucault" in Eric Patterson and Timothy J. Demy, *Philosophers on War* (Newport, RI: Stone Tower Books, 2017), 219-312.

they actually are, and conviction is added to truth by solid justifications, knowing and practicing what is true can be personally liberating. If truth is bound by the highest form of love, namely, *agape* love, that is, committing our will to the true good of others on a consistent basis, then our world will be a better place.

Conclusion

Thinking with excellence involves the pursuit of truth. If you want to stand out among your fellow college and university students, go beyond what you and your family ever imagined possible, and succeed in thought, life, and legacy, then you must be a lover of truth. People will be warring for your mind and heart; they will want you to agree with them, to follow them, and support them with their own agendas, dreams, follies, plans, and purposes. Others don't even know how to raise the right questions, how to discern what is truly true and what is not; they will need your protection. They just follow what others do because they have not been taught differently. Finally, ideas have consequences, and some of those ideas, for better or for worse, are powerful (e.g., Communism). But here are seven reasons that should motivate you to be a lover of truth.

Therefore, when you analyze truth-claims and embrace what may be determined as "true truth," then you will...

1 Be fortified by truth against forces that will war against your heart and mind – it will prove more difficult to exploit you;

2 Live for what truly matters;

3 Be more easily trusted by others;

4 Be less controlled by personal feelings, certain desires, or others (e.g., peer pressure);

5 Stand out as a leader;

6 Be strengthened against mere conjecture, arbitrary rules, and power games;

7 Be able to leave a legacy worth leaving.

"One word of truth outweighs the entire world."

—ALEKSANDR SOLZHENITSYN

LIFESAVING TIPS

"Why Do I Have to Take Liberal Arts Courses?

"Why can't I just take classes that will practically benefit my future?
History, philosophy, religion, and sociology classes are useless!"

Every semester we hear this question, whether by students, parents, or friends. Jokes fly such as, "What is the major difference between a philosopher and a large pizza? A large pizza can feed a family of four." But seriously, why study or even major in the liberal arts tradition? How will an art, language, literature, history, philosophy, and religion course practically benefit us? Consider the following five reasons:

1   By learning from our past, we are able to critically anticipate, meet, and solve problems that continue to find expression in our society. We all stand upon the shoulders of others. We need to know our past to understand how people have dealt with problems that emerge in new generations. Like George Santayana famously observed, "Those who cannot remember the past are condemned to repeat it."

2   By learning how to critically analyze ideas and the consequences that flow which impacts our homes, communities, and our world, we are able to promote and stand against ideas that will either enrich or extract the best parts from us and future generations. We need to think about ideas critically; they can be powerful and lead us to places we have never imagined.

3   By learning what is relevant to other people groups, what they believe, value, and attempt to live out, we will be in a strategic position to better engage them in a qualitative way. People are different. Thus liberal arts raise our social consciousness, help us appreciate others, who they are,

their uniqueness, their struggles, and their contributions to our global society. When ignorance is replaced with knowledge, our biases are challenged, our visions enlarged, and our personal experiences enriched.

4   The cultivation of intellectual habits. If we will proactively engage and assimilate the riches that flow from a liberal arts education (e.g., art; history; literature; philosophy; sociology), then we will be nourished in the most dynamic ways, giving us practical critical thinking skills we can use no matter where we are, what we are doing, or where we are going. We will be able to engage a wide array of complexities, contexts, moral, political, and social issues, people groups, and cultural, moral, and social problems with greater empathy and understanding. We will participate in a rich tradition that finds its origins in culture, reflects and mirrors culture, predicts where culture might be going, and advances personal and social change. Also, we will better understand who we are, what we personally believe, and how our particular environment, situational setting, or ever-changing context feeds us and how we feed on our environment. Hence, the practical skills gained from *Thinking with Excellence* contribute toward this aim.

5   Lastly, a liberal arts education can temper some of the cutting edges of science whereby different powers and technologies in scientific realms of biology, computer science (e.g., social utilities), chemistry, and physics are used to create, abuse, or manipulate our environment, our humanity, and our society. Like *Jurassic Park's* author Michael Crichton warned us, "Your scientists were so preoccupied with whether or not they *could*, that they didn't stop to think if they *should*."

Indeed, a liberal arts education is able to give a cultural, moral, and social voice to science, bring to bear those who have been abused, exploited and marginalized, and scrutinize scientific ideas and achievement in an effort to bring out the best in our humanity, nature, and preserve the riches of our past. How? We are able to draw from vast resources of our historical lessons learned (e.g., art; literature; history), critical thinking skills obtained (e.g., philosophy), empathy, perspective, and a particular sensitivity gained from the bi-relationships between our humanity and our culture (e.g., languages; sociology; religious studies). Moreover, we are able to share our concerns, our hopes, and ideas through the arts (e.g., art; music; film), imagination (fictional literature), and other cultural activities. Like Scottish political activist Andrew Fletcher once stated, "Let me write the songs of a nation – I don't care who writes its laws." Consequently, we are to give careful scrutiny, reflection, and advance what will safeguard who we are, what we are doing, and where we are going; science alone will not do.

"The purpose of history is to explain the present –
to say why the world around us is the way it is.
History tells us what is important in our world,
and how it came to be. It tells us what is to be ignored,
or discarded. That is true power – profound power.
The power to define a whole society."

—MICHAEL CRICHTON

CHAPTER SEVEN

Lead with Logic

"The greatest kindness one can render to any man
consists in leading him from error to truth..."

—Saint Thomas Aquinas

O ne of the most neglected aspects of contemporary education is training to think logically. In fact, for many of us, we were not introduced to logical thinking outside of doing math. But if we can be equipped in basic logical thinking skills, then we will have a powerful set of tools in not only discovering what is "true truth," but we will also develop the sharp ability to discern logical fallacies that pervade every aspect of our society. For example, consider the following 10 popular truth-claims people make:

"There is no truth!"
"All truth is relative!"
"You can't know the truth!"
"It's true for you and not for me!"
"No one has the truth."

"There are no absolutes!"

"That's just your view!"

"All truth depends upon your own perspective!"

"You shouldn't judge!"

"You can only know truth by experience!"

When we apply logic to these truth-claims, we discover they have no logical strength. In fact, they are logically self-defeating. In other words, when we apply logic to those statements, we discern that these statements refute themselves:

"There is no truth!" This is self-contradictory because the person is making a truth-claim. We might simply say, "Is that true?"

"All truth is relative." If we apply logic to this statement, then we discover that this claim is not a relative claim but an objective one. It is self-defeating since we can respond by stating, "Is that a relative truth?"

"You can't know the truth." This is a self-defeating statement since one is claiming to know something about the truth. All we would need to do is ask the question, "Then how do you know that?"

"It's true for you but not for me." If we apply logic to this truth-claim, it is also self-defeating because it implies that it is objectively true that something is "true for you but not for me."

"No one has the truth." An individual is claiming to know something about the truth, namely, no one has the truth. But if we apply logic, we see that this truth-claim is self-contradictory. All we have to say is, "How do you know that is true?"

"There are no absolutes!" Applying logic to this claim it becomes clear that this is an absolute claim. We could reply to this truth-claim by stating, "Are you 'absolutely' sure about that?"

"That's just your view!" Applying logic to this claim, we could say, "Well, that's just your view that this is just my view." See, the statement implies that your truth-claim is relative. But if you relativize that person's response, then it shows how that too is merely personal opinion; it has no logical strength.

"All truth depends on your perspective!" If we apply logic to this truth-claim, then we immediately see that this is an objective statement. We could reply, "Does the claim, 'all truth depends on your perspective' depend on your perspective?"

"You shouldn't judge!" This truth-claim is also contradictory because one who makes this claim is judging as well. We might retort, "If it is wrong to judge, then why are you judging me?"

"You should be tolerant of all views." This truth-claim is also self-contradictory if tolerance means that all views are equally valid. If so, then we could respond with this question, "Then why don't you tolerate my view?"

Therefore, it should be obvious to each of us why knowing and applying logic is critical to thinking with excellence. We all make mistakes in reasoning. Logical reasoning is able to help sort out beliefs from truths. We can have contradictory beliefs, but contradictory truths are logically impossible.

But if we learn to be more careful, precise with our wording, and logical in our thinking, we will indeed have incredible skills to think with excellence. In fact, we contend that if we will learn basic skills of logic and use them in our class discussions, conversations, and papers, then we will gain practical skills that will only help us become all that we can be.

"We can't avoid reasoning; we can only avoid doing it well."

—Peter Kreeft

What is Logic?[28]

Pivotal in classic education and central to computer science, math, and rhetoric, logic involves principles that govern how we should think and speak. Logic means investigating correct reasoning; it is the study of right reason, an ordering, of how to think rightly, or how to find truth. Logic is the way to think so that we come to correct conclusions. Logic also helps us in understanding implications and errors people make in thinking.

When you make a logical argument, you are not asking one to quarrel. No, what you mean by logical argumentation is supporting a truth-claim with logical reasoning. Developing skills in logical thinking will only aid you no matter your discipline or vocation in life, the news you examine, the people you listen to, and the conversations you make. You will have some incredible skills when engaging mesmerizing personalities, authority figures, and various ideas that gain popularity in our communities.

While we highly encourage you to study logic sometime during your undergraduate experience, even if only as an elective, what will help you just as much is understanding and applying the following first principles of logic.

"If you don't build your dream,
someone else will hire you to help them build theirs."

—DHIRUBHAI AMBANI

---

[28] Mortimer J. Adler, *Aristotle for Everybody* (New York: Simon & Schuster, 1978), 129-150; J. P. Moreland and William Lane Craig, *Philosophical Foundations for a Christian Worldview*, 2nd ed. (Downers Grove, IL: 2017), 28-58.

Important Logic Terms to Know[29]

While logical thinking can be quite intimidating because its term is foreign to us, here are some basic terms you need to know if you want to think with excellence.

Counter-arguments: These are challenges and criticisms of an argument.

Deduction: Inferring with necessity a particular conclusion from general premises.

Fallacy: An error in reasoning or a mistaken inference.

Induction: Inferring with probability a general conclusion from particular premises.

Inference: A movement in thought which draws a conclusion from premises.

Premise: Principle upon which an argument is based.

Proof: In a deductive argument, a proof is a sequence of steps, each according to an acceptable rule of inference, to the conclusion to be proved.

Self-evident: Obvious without proof or argument.

Syllogism: A deductive argument with two premises and a conclusion. For example:

1 If I learn philosophical aesthetics, then I will create better works of art (If P, then Q).

2 If I create better works of art, then I can enrich the collective life of the community in the most dynamic ways (If Q, then R).

3 Therefore, if I learn philosophical aesthetics, then I can enrich the collective life of the community in the most dynamic ways (Therefore, if P, then R).

---

[29] McInerny, Peter K. *Introduction to Philosophy* (New York: HarperCollins Publishers, 1992), 5-8; Moore and Bruder. *Philosophy*, 9-10; See also Antony Flew, *A Dictionary of Philosophy*, 2nd ed. (New York: St. Martin's Press, 1979).

"Bad reasoning as well as good reasoning is possible;
and this fact is the foundation of the practical side of logic."

—Charles Sanders Peirce

First Principles of Logical Thinking[30]

What is a "first principle of logic?" In essence, a first principle of logic is a foundational, self-evident logical law of reality. In fact, nothing is more basic to proper logical reasoning than first principles of logic; knowledge can't be known apart from them. Thus, first principles of logic are critical, essential, necessary, and vital to all knowledge.[31] But once we know what they are and how they work, we can use them in every evaluation. Philosopher Norman L. Geisler puts it this way, "If logic is a way to think so that we find truth, then we always ought to be logical so that we know the truth."[32]

We are indebted to Aristotle who helped us to understand what these first principles of logic are.[33] While there are other first principles of logical thinking, consider the following five: Law of Identity; Law of Existence; Law of Non-Contradiction; Law of Excluded Middle; Law of Rational Interference. Let's a take a closer look at them:

Law of Identity (A = A). If x is true, then x is true: An object is identical to itself. For example, all canines are mortal. What do you mean by canine? Or a honeybee is a honeybee. Thus, _____ must be identical to itself. If it were not, then it would not be itself.

Law of Existence (A is). Something exists. For example, I exist. If I didn't exist, then I could not deny my existence.

Law of Non-Contradiction (A is not Non-A). Two contradictory statements cannot be true in the same way and in the same sense. It cannot be a

---

30 Anthony Kenny, *Oxford History of Western Philosophy* (New York: Oxford University Press, 1994), 33-34.

31 Adler, *Aristotle for Everybody*, 140-150.

32 Norman L. Geisler and Ronald M. Brooks, *Come, Let Us Reason: An Introduction to Logical Thinking* (Grand Rapids, MI: Baker, 1990), 14.

33 Idem.

hailstorm and not a hailstorm above my home right now in the same way and in the same sense. Direct opposites cannot be the same. A canine cannot be a canine and not a canine in the same way in the same sense. To deny the law of non-contradiction is to deny reality.

Law of Excluded Middle (Either A or Non-A). A statement is either true or false or either being or non-being. Either statement x is true, or its opposite is true. Either it is snowing outside my window, or it is not snowing outside my window. Further, just because two things have something in common does not mean that they have everything in common. Moreover, there is nothing in between. But leading with logic also means avoid certain logical fallacies that are commonly made.

Law of Rational Inference (A=B & B=C, Therefore A=C). All canines are mortal. Lassie is a canine. Therefore, Lassie is a mortal.

> "There is no greater impediment to the advancement
> of knowledge than the ambiguity of words."
>
> —THOMAS REID

The first principles of logic are self-evident and undeniable. First, they are self-evident; they are immediately and obviously known to us even before we can explain why they are true. And second, the first principles of logic are undeniable for one can't argue against them without implicitly using them. For example, if someone says, "There are no facts; we only have opinions!" One could respond by saying, "Is that a fact or is that only your opinion?" It is safe to conclude that you can't argue against the first principles of logic without using the first principles of logic.

10 Common Fallacies in Logical Thinking[34]

A fallacy is an argument that is logically defective because the premises fail to provide support for the conclusion. Below are ten common fallacies

---

[34] See *www.logicalfallacies.info.; Moore and Bruder, Philosophy, 11-13.*

we often observe in articles, books, conversations, news sources, and a wide array of debates, podcasts, and speeches:

1   **Character Attack (*ad hominem* fallacy).** This occurs when we attack the person and not evaluate the argument. For example, "Her claim can't be right because she is a woman." Never attack the person; always evaluate the argument. Character attacks are inflammatory; they only advance incivility. In the end, no one wins.

2   **Genetic Fallacy.** Related to a character attack, this fallacy contends that truth-claims should not be believed because of their source(s); the arguments are never evaluated on their own terms. For example, this fallacy is committed when we make claims like "Never listen to a Democrat." "Fox News can't be correct in any news analysis because they are a politically conservative news source."

3   **Appeal to Antiquity.** This fallacy takes place when one claims that older truth-claims are true over and against recent ones. For example, "Postmodernism is a recent philosophical movement. Therefore, postmodernism is false." "Intelligent Design Movement is a recent movement against the explanatory power of evolution. Therefore, Intelligent Design Movement is false."

4   **Appeal to Novelty.** This fallacy happens when we say something is true because it is new over and against older ones. For example, "Evolution is the most recent development in biology. Therefore, evolution is true."

5   **Appeal to Authority.** This fallacy takes place when we appeal to a certain authority (e.g., author; celebrity; leader; scholar; thinker) as justification for believing something to be true rather than evaluating the argument on its own strength. "If Richard Dawkins says it, then it must be true." "My professor agrees with what you are saying; you must be right."

6   **Appeal to Force.** This logical fallacy occurs when we appeal to threats to persuade people rather than the logical force of an argument. For example, "If you don't believe what I believe, I will fail you in this course." "If you don't agree with me, then I will no longer be your friend."

7   **Bandwagon Fallacy.** This logical fallacy finds expression when we appeal to the emerging popularity of a particular idea or truth-claim as justification for believing it to be true. But the popularity of a particular idea or truth-claim does not make it necessarily true. For example, "More and more people are doing mushrooms for enlightenment. Therefore, enlightenment must be happening from doing mushrooms."

8   **Straw-Man Fallacy.** This fallacy comes about when one creates, distorts, exaggerates, or misrepresents an argument by substituting the actual argument with a false one. After a false one is created, that is, the "straw-man," the person committing the fallacy tears it down, stating that he or she demonstrated that the argument is fallacious. For example, "Biology professor affirms that all things evolve." A student claims in response, "I can't ever believe that we came from pond scum." A student claims, "I believe there are good reasons and evidences to believe in God's existence!" Professor retorts using the straw-man fallacy, "But Christians believe in the reliability of the Bible. Thus, God does not exist."

9   **False Dilemma.** This fallacy transpires when a false dilemma is given, i.e., when one argues that there are only two choices when at least there is another option available. For example, Socrates committed this false dilemma when he claimed in Plato's *Euthyphro*, (1) "If we say something is good because God wills it, then what is good is arbitrary" or (2) "If we say that God wills something because it is good, that is, what is good or bad is independent of God, then there are moral values independent of God." In other words, God Himself is submitting to moral values that exist independent of Him. But this is a false dilemma because there is a third option available, namely, God wills something to be good because by His very nature He is good. Thus, this is a false dilemma for a third and rational alternative is available.

10   **Hasty Generalization Principle.** This fallacy crops up when one creates a general rule from a single case. For example, "My neighbor's dog is easily provoked to attack humans. Therefore, all dogs are easily provoked to attack humans." "This philosophy book is mind-numbing. Therefore, all philosophy is mind-numbing."

"Think twice before you speak, because your words and influence
will plant the seed of either success or failure in the mind of another."

—NAPOLEON HILL

Logic Adds Conviction to Truth

While there are other aspects of logic that we all should seek to know
and many other fallacies to avoid, the more you practice the first principles of logic, identify, and pro-actively avoid the logical fallacies that
pervade our culture, conversations, and posts on social utilities, the
greater your capabilities to think with excellence and navigate through
the ever-changing dynamics of our society. If you combine logical thinking
with correspondence view of reality, the tests of coherence, evidences,
existential significance, workability, and viability, then you will have the
skills to rise beyond what you ever thought possible in critical thinking
skills. Why? Logic adds conviction to truth.

A Warning

Logic possesses significant force in analysis and conversation. But a warn-
ing is needed. While you are highly encouraged to develop logical thinking
skills to flourish in the most dynamic ways, logic has "teeth." When care-
lessly used against others, it can generate much embarrassment, foster
disunity, and rupture friendships.

"Logic has made me hated in the world."

—PETER ABELARD

Conclusion

While logic is necessary to know and use, especially if you want to think with excellence and cultivate the virtue of prudence; use logic wisely and cautiously when in dialogue with others. Prudence is simply doing the right thing at the right time, in the right way, and for the right reason. Therefore, before you speak, ask what will happen if you point out logical fallacies or incoherent thinking others have committed. But in your own personal development, critical analyses, and in defense of good ideas in the public square, logic is powerful.

> "Consequently, he who wishes to attain to human perfection, must therefore first study Logic, next the various branches of Mathematics in their proper order, then Physics, and lastly Metaphysics."
>
> —MAIMONIDES

LIFESAVING TIPS

"Why Am I Struggling with Doubt?"[35]

Many students we come across struggle with doubt. Doubt affects the educated and uneducated, the rich and the poor; it is a feeling of uncertainty or lack of conviction. Doubters are those who struggle with indecisions, hesitations, and even fears. They feel uncertain about their abilities, what they are learning, what they know, their circumstances, and even who they are. To be sure, these types of doubters are not following after Rene Descartes by using doubt as a helpful tool to find 100% certainty, that which cannot be doubted. No, they struggle with doubt in a very different way. We've discovered that there are three types of doubt, namely intellectual, volitional, and emotional.

Intellectual doubters are not as common as one would think. They are searching for answers to their questions. Some intellectual doubters are struggling with non-willful ignorance; they may not know how to look for the answers or even what to do. Others are suspicious about answers, given competing, rival truth-claims, asking questions like, "How do we know which answer or conclusion is right?" But intellectual doubt is eased when facts are separated from opinions, impressions, and feelings by applying critical thinking skills, especially tests of knowledge you have already learned in *Thinking with Excellence* (e.g., sevenfold criteria for evaluating truth-claims and worldviews; the application of logic). To be sure, not all explanations possess equal weight. Unhurried analysis and careful observations need to be applied and fixed biases and fluid-like influences need to be checked, understood, and accounted for. If the community is involved in the pursuit of answers, they can offer checks and balances

---

[35] We are indebted to the insights of Gary Habermas, *Dealing with Doubt* (Chicago: Moody Press, 1990) who helped us understand the dynamics associated with doubt.

against personal presuppositions and moldable influences, especially those involved in collaborative engagements and cross-disciplinary professional studies.

Volitional doubt tends to be people who have a disposition of doubt; it doesn't matter what the issues are, their circumstances, or the various people they engage, volitional doubters remain skeptical. While doubt may be part of a person's nature, the way they process life, in general, they doubt everything and everyone. While this is a very small group of people, the best way to deal with doubt is to learn how to manage this disposition of doubt in daily living. This requires disciplined thinking and self-control. Instead of attempting to be liberated from doubt, which is part and parcel of who they are, they need to learn how to control it.

But the vast majority of those we encounter are those who struggle with emotional doubt. Though it can often be cloaked in intellectual doubt, emotional doubters see their circumstances, themselves, or others through a poor set of beliefs. Emotional doubt is often evidenced in charged emotional statements like, "No one can answer these questions I have!" These beliefs, while they may be very incoherent and not match up to reality as it is, can generate significant pain within. But the solution is found in replacing the poor set of beliefs that are generating a false view of things, with a better set of beliefs, that is, those that match up to reality as it is, embodying what is good, true, and beautiful. Discipline thinking will also be necessary because these bad beliefs can be so ingrained that they become a habituated way of seeing and doing. But if one will be intentional in focusing on those better beliefs that harmonize with reality as it is, then alleviation from emotional doubt can be realized.

> "Truth, like gold, is to be obtained not by its growth,
> but by washing away from it all that is not gold."
>
> —LEO TOLSTOY

CHAPTER EIGHT

Be a Lover of Truth

"I refuse to accept the view that mankind is so tragically bound
to the starless midnight of racism and war that the bright daybreak
of peace and brotherhood can never become a reality... I believe that
unarmed truth and unconditional love will have the final word."

—Martin Luther King, Jr

Several years ago I (Paul) was invited to a wonderful Sunday luncheon at a very nice Seafood restaurant in Houston. The only seat available was next to this fella who had an obvious disdain for me. These things happen. Not everyone will accept us as we are. But in front of thirteen other people, he turned to me and said, "I've figured out why I don't like you." I said, "Okay?" He replied, "Over my years of experience I've discovered that there are two types of mature Christians, those who are 'trained' and those who are 'well-learned.' You are well-learned; I am trained." Without getting angry, I responded, "So, what you are saying is that you are a product of indoctrination and I am a lover of truth."

Not only did my comment surprise him, but it also facilitated a rich conversation, a teachable moment for all involved.

The problem was that this gentleman found himself struggling with and negatively reacting to words and ideas that were either counter to, never addressed, or mocked by his mentor. But it wasn't merely the terms I used or the way I expressed them. See, the reason why he disliked me and my teaching was that he had embraced the worldview of his mentor, a man he sat under for many, many years. In essence, his basic problem was that he was not a lover of truth, but a lover of his mentor's teachings. Because his mentor taught him what to believe, which he readily received without critical analysis (which we tend to do with people we trust and love), he not only habitually observed and judged all things from this indoctrinated mindset, but he was also self-identified and characterized as a follower of his mentor. Consequently, when he was exposed to words or ideas foreign to him, instead of working through the intellectually and emotional tension he was experiencing with a disposition of understanding, he dismissed, mocked, and resented me.

> "The task of the modern educator is not to cut down jungles
> but to irrigate deserts."
>
> —C. S. LEWIS

Indoctrination is the saturation of another with instruction to the extent that it becomes one's world, one's habituated way of seeing and doing. While we can empathize with the struggles that flow from indoctrination, we must go beyond the well-intended instruction to actually become a lover of truth whereby we welcome truth-claims anyone has to offer, no matter the uniqueness of vocabulary, cultural context, educational background, gender, or race.

A lover of truth will pursue truth no matter where it is found or who proclaims it. The disposition of a lover of truth is one of honest inquiry, a curious thoughtfulness bound by a disposition of personal charity, civility, and humility. In fact, in this day of hyper-partisanship, as thinkers of excellence, we will stand out among so many if we can cultivate an openness, a welcoming, friendly disposition to hear someone out without making premature judgments, a kindness that transcends in both our words and our touch. From this disposition of earnest courtesy, politeness, and respect, we are able to establish a platform of personal credibility, a bridge of interpersonal relationships that will not only allow us to see from another's eyes and learn more from another's perspective but also engender mutual understanding and social healing. Learning from each other can bring about personal and social healing. Dr. Ravi Zacharias, for example, who has traveled the world many times over, and has made relationships with the poor and the rich, the common and the powerful, and the oppressed and the oppressors, repeatedly says, quoting an Indian proverb his mother would share, "Once you've cut off a person's nose, there's no point giving them a rose to smell."

Quite frankly, indoctrination is all too commonplace in the life of the organized community. But if we can recapture the wonder of truth, then our world becomes the classroom, conversations become an art, relationships are forged, and a life of adventure begins. In fact, from such a platform of credibility, civility in conversation, debate, and friendships that transcend differences can be ours. Obstruction, ridicule, and rejection of those who think and communicate differently will be foreign to our personal character and our way of life.

"We become what we behold."

—Marshall McLuhan

How Do You Know if You Are a Product of Indoctrination?

How do you know if you are a product of indoctrination?[36] Consider the following indicators. If these fifteen "road signs" are true in your life, then you are perhaps a product of indoctrination. While there is a time for instruction, we must move from indoctrination to becoming people who think with excellence.

---

[36] Thinking about being a lover of truth vs. being a product of indoctrination came out of a conversation I had (Paul) about what is the difference between those who are "well-learned" and those who are "well-trained." See *www.prshockley.org*.

You Are a Product of Indoctrination if...

☐ You only represent what you have been taught to the extent that you are unwilling to consider any other possible viewpoint seriously.

☐ You habitually see and interpret all other views through your instructor's teachings. In fact, it is difficult for you even to trust any other authority, institution, or person.

☐ Your conversations and your studies are spent articulating, discussing, instructing, programming, and re-hashing what you have been taught. As a result, you honestly refuse to thoughtfully consider any other teaching, point of view, or reference.

☐ You find it difficult to think beyond or outside of your instructor's teaching. Any other category of thought or method is foreign to you. In fact, any other word, idea, term, or word used beyond your instructor is an intellectual and emotional struggle; you are unable to wrap your mind around it. Consequently, you react to the struggle with willful ignorance. You reject what you cannot understand instead of trying to work through it.

☐ You identify yourself (or others fairly define you) with the source of (or beliefs of) that indoctrination. Thus, you are a committed follower of _____.

☐ You readily dismiss any other presentation without honest intellectual inquiry. You will not only refuse to listen to someone different, but you might also mock the presenter.

☐ You take it personally and reject others if they disagree with you.

☐ You do not question your own mentor's truth-claims. Rather, you readily accept it as being truth without critically examining one's justifications. In fact, even one's opinions become "doctrine" to you.

☐ You are unsupportive of those who think differently from you.

☐ You tend to misrepresent, mock, or even ridicule other views and those that believe or proclaim them.

☐ If you are honest with yourself, you are fearful to investigate what lies beyond what you have been taught to believe. Thus, you cloak fear with dogmatism.

☐ You tend to alienate those you know and love if they have been hurt or damaged by either the source of or the implications that flow from that indoctrination.

☐ Cult-like symptoms emerge. For example, you only promote and proclaim your mentor's lessons and literature. All other materials are unacceptable or are held with suspicion. In fact, you may even refuse to quote another source than what your instructor has produced or even your mentor refuses to quote another source other than his own material.

☐ Even when your instructor has moved on, become discredited or even has passed away, you tend to live in the glory of the past with nostalgic sentiments while opportunities and possibilities slip away from you.

☐ You equate intellectual and moral maturity with the amount of saturation of your mentor's teaching.

> "Thirst is made for water; inquiry for truth."
>
> —C. S. Lewis

Rather than being a product of indoctrination, *Thinking with Excellence* demands being one who pursues the truth. As you come to know what is true, conforming yourself to the truth in daily living, you will go beyond what you ever thought possible. Why? People are longing for truth, for something to believe in that is true and trustworthy. Thus, if you seek to know, practice, and protect what is true and trustworthy, flowing from a disposition of personal integrity that generates credibility, civility, and humility before others, then you will make your life count for something great. You will touch lives in the most meaningful way.

You Are (or Have Become) a Lover Of Truth if...

☐ You value truth over personality, power, or skills of persuasion.

☐ You uphold intellectual honesty over and against closed-mindedness.

☐ You pursue a broad education – you go beyond the beliefs and personalities of your subculture.

☐ You experience surprising insights as you discover truth in extraordinary ways.

- ☐ You make interpersonal relationships with people who are not only different from you but who also may disagree with you.
- ☐ You possess a certain attractiveness that will be distinguishable – you are able to look and listen for and offer truth that goes beyond programmed instruction and propaganda.
- ☐ You cherish an adventurous life – your pursuit of truth enlightens you in ways you have never considered.
- ☐ You develop competence and creative insight as you engage others rather than simply repeating what you cherish as true.
- ☐ Your scope of relationships continually enlarges as you engage others. People complement you and add to your understanding, practice, and protection of the truth.
- ☐ You practice truth and love and love and truth because you recognize the inseparable valuable of both. You recognize that *Agape* love is the commitment of the will to the true good of another person.
- ☐ You realize the consequences of ideas in the marketplace of ideas. Good ideas have good consequences, and bad ideas have bad consequences.
- ☐ You appreciate viable, reasonable options within the range of reasonable possibilities.
- ☐ You avoid presumptuous, premature thinking, and the resultant costly mistakes.
- ☐ You refute what is false with what is true, and not merely with indoctrination. You justify your truth-claims and not merely quote your mentor.
- ☐ You promote personal charity, politeness, and humility, not unnecessary criticism.
- ☐ You occasionally and habitually ask questions to any truth-claim such as "What do you mean by this? How did you come to that conclusion?" Questions such as "Why? Where? How? When? To What Extent?"
- ☐ You pursue knowledge no matter the source.
- ☐ You reject the vices such as apathy and willful ignorance; these concepts are foreign to you.
- ☐ You experience the joy of personal discovery of truth rather than relying upon another's interpretation of it.

Conclusion

One of the greatest benefits of thinking with excellence will be rising above mere indoctrination, as valuable as it may have been in our formative years, to becoming an individual who prizes truth. Even though it will not eliminate criticism by those who are in your spheres of living, it will propel you to excellence and promote inter-personal relationships that enable you to make a life-giving difference. You will be commended, your community enriched, and your legacy left behind will be treasured.

The Seven Sins according to Mahatma Gandhi:

"Wealth without work
Pleasure without conscience
Knowledge without character
Commerce without morality
Science without humanity
Religion without sacrifice
Politics without principle."

If we could add three more to Gandhi's list of sins it would be:

Tongue without wisdom
Truth without love
Love without truth.

LIFESAVING TIPS

"How Do I Make Myself More Marketable/Qualified for a Future Career?"

Standing out in a crowd sometimes is not as easy as it seems. The job market can be competitive and gathering enough experience sometimes seems daunting or challenging. The good news is that there are steps you can take to make yourself more marketable/qualified for a future career. Here are **six suggestions** to maximize your college experience:

1   **Complete an Undergraduate Research Project.** Most university programs have opportunities for undergraduate research. This provides college students with additional study working closely with a faculty mentor. In many cases, all you need to do is ask a professor in person or via email. They will be able to tell you whether they have an opportunity and they also will be able to guide you.

2   **Enroll in University Honors.** If you are a go-getter and you strive for excellence (or even if you don't yet but want to strive towards your fullest potential) consider enrolling in university honors. This is a prestigious program available at most universities where you complete additional projects and work closely with faculty mentors. Information related to such a program should be available on a university webpage or within a department.

3   **Join a club related to your field.** Joining a club or organization of interest always is a great idea to learn more outside the classroom and is a beneficial way to meet other students who have the same interests. Clubs often lead to extracurricular opportunities that not only enrich your college experience but also provide you with valuable resume-building material.

4 **Inquire about an observation opportunity.** Sometimes the best way to build experience in your area of interest (and future career prospects) is to seek opportunities to observe in the field. This can be simply shadowing a hospital nurse or a dentist in private practice. These are all people who can eventually provide letters of recommendation or can open a door for you (perhaps provide you with a valuable professional reference that lands you a job!).

5 **Volunteer in your area of interest.** Volunteering not only builds character but also looks good to potential employers. There are several volunteer opportunities in each community and finding the right fit is a phone call (or an online search) away.

6 **Stay healthy.** Unfortunately, first impressions matter! If you don't take care of yourself physically, emotionally, mentally, etc., then it could keep others from taking a "second look" at you. Do your best to stay fit in every area of your life.

> "Working hard is very important. You're not going
> to get anywhere without working extremely hard."
>
> —GEORGE LUCAS

CHAPTER NINE

What's My Major: Major in Life-Long Learning!

"Education is what remains after one has forgotten
what one has learned in school."

—ALBERT EINSTEIN

When we are young, most of us dream about what we want to become in our adult lives. Some of us may be adults and still in the process of trying to figure out our dreams – or maybe just what our plans are for the next day. One thing is for sure, nothing is guaranteed. In many instances, we may think we have it all planned, but a life event, epiphany, family emergency, or even a change of our minds may guide us down a different path of circumstances. It has been said that life happens when we are busy making other plans. And it's also been said that life is too short, you only live once, and live life to the fullest. So much pressure! How do I get it right? Well, the answer perhaps is that it's not about getting it right, but about learning from your life experiences.

An Unexpected Life Change. When I (Raul) began my college journey, I thought I had it all figured out. The stars were aligned, and everything pointed towards majoring in vocal performance. I had just completed a high school journey of choral and solo competitions as well as all-state choir honors and invited singing gigs that included performing for notable people like then Texas Governor George Bush. I had songs, such as the National Anthem, ready to sing any time including a full repertoire of classical *arias* and other church solos and hymns. I sang in the car, sang in the shower, sang all day and every day at home (my brother was thrilled), and sang randomly in public places, which usually followed with a range of reactions. My voice landed me a significant scholarship to attend Trinity University in San Antonio. In college, I continued my musical pursuits and did well within my major. I eventually added a double degree in business administration (to ease the concerns of my parents and follow their advice of having "something to fall back on") and graduated with both a music and business degree. For my final undergraduate recital, I sang Schumann's *Dichterliebe* and made the decision to add a set of Spanish love songs at the end, because I knew my family and friends would need a good finale to get them over the fact that they just had to sit through an hour of 16 songs in German!

Once I completed my undergraduate degrees, I moved to Longmont, Colorado and began studying towards a master's degree in vocal performance and pedagogy at the University of Colorado-Boulder. I'll never forget the day I received the acceptance letter in the mail. I remained focused on my dream of singing professionally and also the added aspiration of teaching voice to others - eventually. At this point in my life, I already knew I wanted to become a college professor someday. Colorado was everything I dreamed of, and more. Beautiful scenery, actual seasons (I was from South Texas and it was my first major experience with snow), and friendly people that walked wherever they wanted to go – including through oncoming traffic and the cars stopped for them! Incredible, I thought to myself. If I tried that in Texas, I would have been the recipient of incessant honking, or worse, run over! And did I mention Colorado was home to more and more singing! I'm pretty certain that I sang my face off, literally. The classes were engaging, and the professors were very knowledgeable and helpful.

My time in Colorado was everything, but something happened to me during my first year in graduate school. As I practiced in the conservatory-like atmosphere, singing became more and more demanding, and my love for performing became laborious. Yet, I practiced daily, trying my best to improve continually. Little did I know that my over-practicing was straining my voice, my livelihood. Singing became difficult, yet I persisted. I was determined. Then came my final voice jury (i.e., final exam) at the end of the year. I was nervous, so much more nervous than my prior jury at mid-year. I sang my best but did notice that my voice was not quite right. There was something wrong with the sound, and this included my speaking voice. After my performance, I waited a few days for my results. I remember getting the call to schedule a meeting with the chair of the voice program. When I walked into her office, I could see in her body language and demeanor that the news I was about to receive that day would not be favorable. The chair paused and then proceeded to tell me that I was placed on academic probation and that I would need to be reconsidered for the program.

It was as though time stood still. Like in the movies when someone experiences pain or a detriment and everything moves in slow motion and the other person's voice sounds muffled and unintelligible. It was just like that. My life changed. I was devastated. Shards of pain began to emanate from my heart. My body (and brain) actually started to hurt. Tears began to stream down my face in front of the voice chair, and I knew I could not speak. If I spoke, my voice would waver and tremble with sadness. The chair was surprisingly comforting at that moment. I remember she reached for a box of tissues and said something to the tune of: "I know what you are feeling and I am here for you. Our voice is a huge part of who we are, and it's difficult to take criticism on such an important part of us."

And she was right. It was one thing to learn the flute and be horrible at playing it. That's just an instrument (no offense, flautists – just trying to prove a point here). But when the instrument is essentially you? I was told that my voice (a huge part of myself) wasn't good enough. And even though I technically had a 4.0 GPA (yes, it's true – and I tried to appeal), I was still placed on academic probation and would have to re-audition to get back into the program.

I made the decision to leave the program – and the state. Other concurrent family events supported that decision at the time. And in hindsight, it's one of the best decisions I made for many reasons. It wouldn't be until later that I would visit a doctor and find out that I had experienced pre-vocal nodules (edema) and mild muscle tension dysphonia. The strain on my vocal folds had caused the condition I had experienced in Colorado. Interestingly, the entire experience led me to my current field of speech-language pathology. Because of that life-changing moment, I found my true passion for working with individuals with communication disorders. And, I'm happy to report that with vocal exercises I was able to improve my speaking and singing voice and that I was able to resume singing. But now I sing because I want to, not because I have to. And my family and friends often ask me to sing for various events as a result.

Therefore, you can have it all figured out (like I did) and things can STILL end up changing. I did not choose the right major – but that was OK. I used the experience as a life lesson and made the most of what remained. And, I used my learned skills as a vocal performer and pedagogue and continued to work with vocal professionals to help them improve their voices. Some might call it a Win-Win in the end. I certainly think so.

Choosing A Major

So What's My Major, Tom? If you are asking who "Tom" is at this moment, it's a reference to the song *Major Tom* from the 80s. It's a song that represents a journey, much like the journey taken in college. At first, things may start off rather smoothly, then there are inevitably obstacles along the way that we encounter and that we must overcome, but, in the end, we finally make it through one way or another. And life goes on. That being said, one of the biggest questions you will have to answer when you are in college will be: "What is my major?"

As you embark on your educational journey, you may not have a definitive idea on what your main area of study will be. It is completely normal if you come to campus and don't know what you want for a career. That's part of the college experience! You can figure it out as you go. Or maybe you do have an idea and that idea changes (that's OK as well). If you know exactly what you plan to do, perhaps you haven't considered a minor that complements your major study. There are many things to consider!

Majors Don't Define You

Start with the Core, Then Look for More

If you are initially uncertain about what to major in, the good news is that there are a group of classes known as the "core" curriculum. Every university has them, and these are classes that all students must take in order to graduate. Classes within a core curriculum include courses such as language and literature (e.g., English), math, history, and science. When in doubt, check with your advisor and get the core classes out of the way! Once you start taking these courses, you will begin to learn more about your interests. Then, you can explore other subjects until you eventually conquer the world.

Explore Different Subjects

Take the time to explore different classes and explore your own interests. See what moves you, fascinates you, drives you, and compels you. You may be surprised at what piques your curiosity. Perhaps it's an astronomy course or an interesting take on philosophy? Maybe you want to learn a foreign language or study forestry? The truth is, you will never have another moment quite like "the now" (your undergraduate experience) to explore varied topics. Sure, you can always go back to school later. Or retire and then find your passion. But why wait until the future? Seize the moment today!

Don't Be Afraid to Do What You Love

Many people are inclined to seek out the glamorous jobs or to acquire occupations that will bring them monetary wealth (all of us can't make it as a social media superstar!). But the truth is, someone wise once said that it is better to be happy in life and do something you love, rather than do something you don't love just to do it. The money won't be worth it in the end. There are always ways to make money, but happiness is created, not earned! Happiness is also not given freely – unless you receive a new puppy. Plus, we need to be realistic about what we can achieve, what we can do, and what strengths fall within our own skill set.

> "Your work is going to fill a large part of your life, and the only way
> to be truly satisfied is to do what you believe is great work.
> And the only way to do great work is to love what you do.
> If you haven't found it yet, keep looking. Don't settle.
> As with all matters of the heart, you'll know when you find it."
>
> —STEVE JOBS

Embrace Your Gift Cluster

As you seek to determine what your interests are, it is important to remember to do so with an accepted understanding of your gift cluster. Your gift cluster is composed of your leadership style, learned abilities and skills (e.g., mathematics; sports), natural gifts and talents (e.g., music), and personality style. Your gift cluster also includes experiences that have shaped who you are, the knowledge you have acquired, and other unique aspects that make you the unique person that you are.

Major in Life-Long Learning!

When it comes down to it, majoring in a particular area in college is just one part of your life. Your educational pursuits should lead to life-long learning. In areas of speech and language, professionals are taught to work with and challenge children just outside of or beyond their abilities – but within reach – in order to stimulate growth (Vygotsky's Zone of Proximal Development[37]). In the same fashion, you should strive for excellence in a way that you are challenged on a daily basis, not only in college but also in life! Stretch your brain! But, remember, you don't have to over-do it! For example, you don't have to lift 200 pounds of weights on the first try in weightlifting. Just like you build endurance with exercise, build intellectual strength over time. Start by reading a few pages of a new book for pleasure just a little bit each day. Before you know it, you will finish a new book in no time! Or maybe, just start with reading your textbook!

There is one more important point worth mentioning about how children learn: they learn from their environment. We are aware that things like prior print awareness (knowledge of books and reading before entering school) predict later reading success. In the same fashion, interactions with adults shape a young person's mind. Phrases that caregivers use, the frequency of new words, good modeling of speech sounds, and exhibiting good social interactions are critical to later success in school. Therefore, surround yourself with people who will make you think intellectually – who will make you better. Choose to spend your time with people who will challenge your own thinking and compel you to grow. Take the chance and overcome any fears you may have now! The more you take control of your college experience, the more you will get out of your education.

---

[37] Pentti, Hakkarainen, Pentti, "The Zone of Proximal Development in Play and Learning" (2018) at *https://www.researchgate.net/publication/265626894_The_zone_of_proximal_development_in_play_and_learning*. Retrieval date: 26 July 2018.

What Is Grad School?

Graduate school is advanced training (beyond an undergraduate program). Traditionally, graduate school occurs after one receives their Bachelor's degree. As you begin your college experience, you are working on your undergraduate degree – which usually is represented with the letters B.A. or B.S. (Bachelor of Arts; Bachelor of Science). This can be in any program offered by your college or university. However, some professions (e.g., medical; social sciences; education) require an advanced degree. These degrees are represented generally by M.A. or M.S. (Master of Arts; Master of Science).

Majors Don't Define You

OK – so you finally chose your major. Wonderful! Now, don't let it define you. What does that mean you might ask? Continue your pursuit of a well-rounded education. Find courses that complement your major area and perhaps consider pursuing a minor. Seek opportunities to learn from others in different fields. Don't stop learning in other areas simply because you've chosen a major. Sometimes plans change or life circumstances cause plans to change. Be a person who excels in their major but who also can carry and hold a conversation in many areas. Surprise people with your vast knowledge of religions, business policy, politics, music history, and international economics!

Conclusion

At the beginning of this chapter, a story was provided demonstrating how circumstances can change our life plans. Plans change, and that's OK. Things happen (whether we want them to or not) and we choose how to react to them. Everyone goes through hardships. Someone else always has it worse than we do. People who can learn from those experiences and move forward have the best chance for making the most of them. Don't sweat the small stuff. Embrace your journey, regardless of the obstacles or outcome. Keep your head high and learn through observations and experiences. Take mental notes. Practice trial and error. Don't be afraid to grow. Walk and let go of the table. Seek advice from others. Unlearn and re-learn concepts. Rise above the strife and the doubt.

"Life is 10% what happens to you and 90% how you react to it."

—CHARLES R. SWINDOLL

LIFESAVING TIPS

"I Don't Know what to Do with My Life?"

This is one of our highest sources of anxiety on college and university campus. Here's our 7-fold response:

1   **You are not alone.** We receive this question every semester from all sorts of students from all walks of life.

2   **Adjust your expectations.** While we are used to receiving immediate answers and fixes to our problems, knowing what you should do takes time, seasoned experience, and evaluated reflection of self.

3   **Learn to hope.** Wisdom must first be cultivated in you so that you may discover what the best thing(s) to do may be. Patience is required. Be patient.

4   **Experimentation is the proving ground.** Experiment, serve, and volunteer in a wide array of interests.

5   **Change.** Don't keep on doing the same thing expecting different results. Try new things; overcome your fears.

6   **Know who you are.** What is your gift cluster? Don't deceive yourself into thinking you can do something that is not in your gift set. Instead, accept who you are and work on developing your natural gifts and talents.

7   **The power of community.** Go beyond meeting your own desires and needs to invest in the lives of others actively. From those inter-personal relationships made via meeting people's practical needs, new paths will open up, affirmations will be engendered, and lessons will be learned.

From doing these seven things, we have seen undiscovered paths taken, a unique "tailoring" take shape, and meaningful destinies forged.

"The aim of all education, is, or should be,
to teach people to educate themselves."

—ARNOLD J. TOYNBEE

CHAPTER TEN

Navigating with Excellence: Taking Care of You

"The price of anything is the amount of life you exchange for it."

—Henry David Thoreau

Most people have good intentions and want the best for themselves. We strive for excellence. We are taught to make the most of our lives and to live for each experience. We are told to be happy. But let's face it: life is hard! Whether it's balancing two jobs and school, raising children as a single parent and managing a career and continuing education, or taking care of elderly parents along with everything else – everyone has a story. We all struggle from time-to-time. Therefore, when life begins to feel heavy, we all need to remember a few things. And while this is not an exhaustive list, there are some important points that need to be discussed. For example, sometimes we just need to remember to breathe!

Taking care of "YOU"

We've all heard the saying "treat others the way you want to be treated." But we don't often ask ourselves, "Hey self, how are you doing?" Our busy lives and hectic schedules usually result in neglecting our basic needs. It's kind of like waiting till the last minute to change the oil in your car or to schedule that health check-up. And, while we are on the subject, please remember to take care of your car and general health! It goes without saying, you should "check-in" with yourself at least a couple of times a week. Pause and reflect. Take time out of your day to do something fun! But have you ever really thought about how you are taking care of yourself?

Some of us are natural givers and often will help others at the expense of our own needs. While giving to others is virtuous, you are the most influential person to your own life! How you treat yourself and how you console yourself will, in part, determine whether you can help others. Helping yourself also will increase the likelihood of whether you have the skills to study effectively for that exam or finish that project with excellence. Sure, we gain much of our influences from others, but it's how we respond to those influences and how we choose to react to them that matters most.

The simple act of being grateful. You will have moments of despair. There will be times that you feel you cannot move forward or that there is just too much to be done and not enough time. It may seem like "the world is out to get you," or you may say to yourself "I can't do this!" In fact, we all go through this, sometimes on a daily basis. We have various ways to cope, but the stress sometimes may feel overwhelming. Relax, you "got" this!

Interestingly, there is evidence that the simple act of being *grateful* goes a long way. For example, you may be grateful that you have a wonderful roommate at school or that you have family close to rely on. Perhaps you are thankful that class was canceled and you have more time to study for another test. Some days we find gratitude in the simple fact that we survived one more day or that the weather outside is beautiful! In his book[38], *The Upward Spiral: Using Neuroscience to Reverse the Course of Depression, One Small Change at a Time*, Dr. Alex Korb discusses the idea that gratitude boosts the neurotransmitter dopamine like the antidepressant Wellbutrin.

---

[38]   See A. Korb, *The Upward Spiral: Using Neuroscience to Reverse the Course of Depression, One Small Change at a Time* (Oakland, CA: New Harbinger Publications, 2015).

He writes:

> "The benefits of gratitude start with the dopamine system,
> because feeling grateful activates the brain stem region that
> produces dopamine. Additionally, gratitude toward others
> increases activity in social dopamine circuits, which makes
> social interactions more enjoyable..."

Therefore, the singular act of being grateful makes us feel better. And if we demonstrate gratitude towards others, it creates more positive relationships. Sounds like a win-win! But there's more. Dr. Korb also points out that you don't even have to find anything to be grateful for, that the simple act of searching is all that matters:

> "It's not finding gratitude that matters most; it's remembering to look
> in the first place. Remembering to be grateful is a form of emotional
> intelligence...[and] as emotional intelligence increases, the neurons
> in these areas [prefrontal cortex] become more efficient. With higher
> emotional intelligence, it simply takes less effort to be grateful."

Gratitude makes significant changes to our brains. It allows us to feel better and focus more on what we are doing. We gain better skills to execute the tasks that need to be completed. Sometimes it heals us and helps us overcome unforeseen obstacles in our lives. So be grateful! Share your gratitude with others. Compliment your friends and family. Be the positivity in the world that you want reflected back upon you!

Learn from the really bad days. Sometimes no matter how grateful we are, we still encounter those tough days where nothing seems to bring us out of our gloom. We may feel guilty, and that guilt may transform into later shame. It is important to remember that it happens to all of us! In fact, shame and guilt activate the brain's reward center, which is why we can sometimes wallow in these emotions. You also might be asking, "What if I'm a worrier?" Interestingly, Dr. Korb discusses in his book the idea that worrying makes our brains feel better because it signifies that we are doing something about the problem and that worrying is better than doing nothing. He also suggests labeling negative feelings and giving the idea of "awfulness" a name (e.g., sad; angry) because "consciously recognizing the emotions reduces their impact." Therefore, be grateful for what you have and when you are worrying about a class project, exam, or perhaps a missed assignment, remember that worrying can be good but couple it with being grateful. If your emotions get the best of you, label your feelings to reduce their impact! And then take action.

Don't Compare Yourself to Others. It is very easy to listen to the successes of others, and have a momentary feeling of jealousy or dream that our lives were different and much like theirs. We wish we could tell you that this changes with time but, sadly, that is not the case. When we consume social media on a daily basis (as most of us do), we see the same thing over and over again: John has another new car; Sarah just shared a post about her third trip to Europe; David has a wonderful life with a white picket fence, a fabulous wife, and two kids; Emily finished school with honors and was accepted to a graduate program at a prestigious university.

The thing to remember is that social media is not real life. It's a projection of our lives controlled by us. We share with the world what we want everyone to see about ourselves. While many individuals choose to play the "victim" or are attention-seekers and post negatively, the majority of us display ourselves in a positive light in most cases. This is also true in the world of academia. Many students around you will present themselves in a positive or negative light. Regardless of what they do, *DO NOT* compare yourself to others. You are your own unique, fantastic self!

Sure, a little healthy competition is good. It makes us better. Applying for that teaching assistantship, for example, or obtaining that competitive work-study position is terrific. It helps us grow. But at the end of the day, if you are looking at the successes of others and comparing yourself to others negatively, that will not be beneficial. Find happiness from within and make the most of your abilities as you search for opportunities that excite you and round out your skills.

One of the things that I (Raul) have taught my children is not to compare themselves to others. On my birthday many years ago, and after enduring the tedious (but rewarding) process of becoming approved as an adoptive parent, I was fortunate to be selected (matched with) and officially adopt my four children (biological siblings) in court. It was a glorious day and one of the best days of my life. I share my birthday with them, and I remind my children that they were (and always will be) the best birthday gifts I have ever received. Coming from foster care, my children already had the odds stacked against them. Mindful of all the reported statistics related to foster children[39] and also aware that mindset is everything, I've done my best to love them unconditionally and to remind them not to let their past define them, but to acknowledge it, accept it, learn from it, and move forward to create a brighter future. When they doubt their abilities (as most children do), I tell my kids that they are worthy, remind them that they were given a second chance at life to make the most of it and that rather than comparing themselves to others, carve their own unique path and own it! Being different is OK. We are all different in our own ways. Let us love ourselves and, as a result, we will become better at loving others.

Be "Good Enough." Whether you are a perfectionist and always want everything to be completely perfect or if you are the type of student that procrastinates, does minimal work, and just barely does enough to "get by," the key to educational success (and beyond) is the idea that you tackle a project, task, exam, speech, and interaction and that you are "good enough" at it. It doesn't have to be perfect. And you certainly should not strive for mediocrity. Making it "good enough" is what you should aim for.

The Problem with Being "Too Happy." Have you ever heard the saying "Too much of a good thing?" Well, it's true. Before you eat that entire quart

---

39 Child Welfare Information Gateway, "Child Welfare Information Gateway 2016. U.S. Department of Health and Human Services, Children's Bureau (2017) at *https:// www.childwelfare.gov/pubs/factsheets/foster/*. Retrieval Date: 26 July 2018.

of ice cream or drink that whole 2-liter of soda, know this: The feeling of happiness will be temporary. You will desire more and more happiness until you get to a point where you require more of a good thing to make you even happier. That one quart of ice cream next time won't be enough anymore. There is always a limit to what we can consume and, eventually, our happiness will run out, and sadness will take over. We discussed the idea that guilt and shame (and wallowing in those emotions) activates the reward center in our brains. This happens with both emotional extremes (happiness and sadness). Therefore, we have to find a balance and accept both moments of happiness (which are good) and sadness (which also are beneficial in learning).

> "The desire for more positive experience is itself a negative experience.
> And, paradoxically, the acceptance of one's negative experience
> is itself a positive experience."
>
> —MARK MANSON

There is such thing as being "too happy."[40] At the same time, when we experience failure, we must try our best to acknowledge it and make it a positive learning experience. There should be a natural balance between the two. The philosopher Alan Watts discusses the idea of Reversed Effort – The Backwards Law. It's the concept that, in many cases, the harder we try, the less we shall succeed. He explains it in the following way: "Muddy water is best cleared by leaving it alone." Therefore, it's the premise that we need a combination of relaxation and effort to do well. When you are studying for a test, for example, take breaks. Pace yourself on that writing assignment. Write in "chunks" and allow your brain time to rest and recover. Remember, balancing your life is everything!

---

[40] Manson, M. *The Subtle Art of Not Giving a F*ck: A Counterintuitive Approach to Living a Good Life.* First edition (New York: HarperOne, 2016).

"The harder we try with the conscious will to do something, the less we shall succeed. Proficiency and the results of proficiency come only to those who have learned the paradoxical art of doing and not doing, or combining relaxation with activity, of letting go as a person in order that the immanent and transcendent unknown quantity may take hold. We cannot make ourselves understand; the most we can do is to foster a state of mind, in which understanding may come to us."

—Aldous Huxley

Other Ways of Taking Care of "YOU"

There are limitless ways we can take care of ourselves. Half the battle is figuring out what works best for us and then making an individualized plan for excellence! The notion of "breaks" may be interpreted in various ways (e.g., exercise; listening to music; taking a nap). Therefore, as you explore what taking care of "you" will ultimately look like, consider the following as examples and then continue your quest in self-discovery as you move towards thinking with excellence.

Visiting with family and visiting home. In all the hustle and bustle of the university experience, we may sometimes forget what the comforts of home may bring to our overall well-being. Regardless of your background and upbringing, there is bound to be someone in your life that brings you joy and comfort. This could be a parent, grandparent, relative, or close friend that is much like a family member. In each of these cases, regular contact with these individuals will provide you with a peace of mind you may not have known existed. In fact, research has shown that the simple act of texting your loved ones on a regular bases increases your chances of excelling in school. It can be a text or a call, whichever you prefer. However, if you are close enough to home, in person also is beneficial, if possible.

Knowing when to say "NO." It is very easy for many of us to be a "yes" person. In a social and educational setting, we want to fit in and show that we are dedicated by offering to do more than perhaps we are able to do. In those moments when you find yourself questioning whether you should agree to take on another club or school activity, for example, consider your current commitments first. It's OK to say "no" in a polite way to offers to do more. Prioritize your time and also *PROTECT YOUR TIME*! Ask yourself how you want to spend your time – and be a little guarded.

Motivating yourself and setting goals. If you don't like doing something and you are forced to do it – surprise, you won't achieve as much from it as you might have hoped. When you set a goal, remain motivated towards it and realize it. Moreover, this will have a better effect on you than if things were just left to happen by chance. This is why college students who are active consumers of their education do better than those who wait for things to be given to them. Find what motivates you. But if you are required to take a course in physics and it's a subject that you do not enjoy, try to find an enjoyable aspect of it. We know, that's sometimes easier said than done. If you can't see an element of the course that is appealing, perhaps revel in the idea that the course isn't going to last forever (maybe that's you being grateful for an end goal!). But motivation goes a long way. For example, if we exercise because we want to, not because we feel like we have to, we will get more out of the experience. Wanting to do something and having to do something yields different results in many cases. You may not want to volunteer for a math club, for example, but may find more joy in volunteering for an animal shelter. Finding what motivates you and making the most of the experience will enrich your life. And don't forget to set goals. Sometimes a simple goal is getting up in the morning and making it to class! Whatever your needs are, make it happen!

There is this thing called Imposter Syndrome. Imposter Syndrome is the feeling we sometimes get when we feel like we don't belong or have the education, experience, knowledge, or skills needed in a particular area. You get the new job, but you just don't quite feel like you have the skills you need to succeed fully. Perhaps you are bicultural, and you don't feel like you fully fit in with a particular cultural group. The truth is, we all suffer from Imposter Syndrome at some point in our lives. It may be an athlete who made the team, but they don't feel they measure up. Or the student who made it into the prestigious school but they don't feel like they are worthy. Remember to "fake it till you make it!" We all do it! You are worthy and you belong!

> "It is impossible to live without failing at something,
> unless you live so cautiously that you might as well not have lived
> at all, in which case you have failed by default."
>
> —J.K. Rowling

Are you a Non-Traditional Student? That's OK!

It's never too late to start school again. You are responsible for your future. While being a non-traditional student may seem overwhelming, you certainly belong in an educational setting. Don't forget about that pesky Imposter Syndrome! Here are some things to remember if you fall under the non-traditional student status:

- Put yourself out there.

- Make friends in class.

- Know you are just as capable as everyone else.

- Keep a balance in your life.

- Make time for yourself and your family.

- Don't give up! Follow your dreams!

When I (Raul) was completing my Ph.D. in Communication Sciences and Disorders, I was working two jobs and also helping out with a daycare on a regular basis. It was overwhelming, but I set aside time for my studies and tried to find the right balance between school, work, and life. Sure, the impulse to give it all up and open an organic soap shop in an antique district was always in the back of my mind – sometimes during more unbearable moments! But my parents had always instilled in me the importance of education, and it was that, along with my motivation to pursue my educational goals that helped me through. While I was completing my Ph.D., I was surprised to learn that my mother had decided she wanted to pursue a doctorate as well. She was obviously older than the average college-age student and would be considered by many a non-traditional student (though she is very youthful in appearance and spirit). Her apprehension to begin her doctoral pursuits later in life did not get in her way, however. Interestingly, she and I ended up graduating at the same time (same semester), and we had a joint graduation celebration. It was such a wonderful moment in our lives. She taught me that it didn't matter what happens in life and what your circumstances were, that you can always go back to school, follow your dreams, and achieve your goals. Remember, you will still learn things from your parents/family members!

Being honest with yourself. This last point cannot be overstated enough. The only way you are truly going to think with excellence and achieve your educational goals is if you are honest with yourself and accept yourself for who you are. Don't try to be someone you are not. Remember, the grass is not always greener on the other side. Perhaps the poet Ovid's version is more meaningful: "The harvest is always richer in another man's field." Don't live life through others when you have your own story to write. You are unique! You can't change everyone, but you can make a difference in other peoples' lives by committing your will to the true good of others.

> "Some think that they know everybody,
> but they really don't know themselves."
>
> —ALBRECHT DÜRER

Once you start your career, you will never really have the chance just to sit and learn all day. You will find yourself perhaps reminiscing about those days and pondering the merit of reliving them, thinking how wonderful would it be to go back and do just that!

Conclusion

In summary, navigating with excellence sometimes requires us to care for ourselves along the way. Check in with yourself! Be grateful for the opportunities in your life. Learn from the bad days and remember to do "good enough" and be OK with it. Lift yourself up and don't compare yourself to others. Avoid the feeling of Imposter Syndrome – you are where you are for a reason, and you are worthy of that spot in college or whatever your endeavor is at the moment. But remember, don't be too happy, be happy with yourself and what you have. Stay in close communication with your family. You need them, and they need you. Don't be afraid to say "no" as respectfully as you can. Set achievable goals for yourself. And, above all, be honest with yourself!

Gandalf, "You've [Bilbo] been sitting quietly for far too long. Tell me, when did doilies and your mother's dishes become so important to you? I remember a young hobbit who was always running off in search of Elves, in the woods. He'd stay out late, come home, after dark, trailing mud and twigs and fireflies. A young hobbit who would've liked nothing better than to find out what was beyond the borders of the Shire. The world is not in your books and maps. It's out there."

—"The Hobbit: An Unexpected Journey."

LIFESAVING TIPS

"What Common Problems Do You See among Students Each and Every Semester?"

Other than not knowing how to read to understand, time management, and forgetting to look at their course syllabus regularly, two problems stand out among students every semester, namely, the problems of diversion and apathy (indifference).

Simply put, diversion is a wide array of anemic distractions that occupy our attention, resources, and time. While students are taking in trivial diversions, trivial diversions are absorbing them. Since time is limited, students end up only giving their "leftovers" to what matters most, namely, their studies. Consequently, being taken in by trivial diversions impacts not only their academic record but also limits their opportunities to be accepted into graduate or professional programs for further education or training (e.g., law; medicine; veterinary science). Unfortunately, many gifted students "fail out" of school altogether, especially when particular diversions become addictive (e.g., gaming; sports).

Blaise Pascal offers striking insight into the problems of diversion. He observed:

He who does not see the vanity of the world is himself very vain. Indeed who do not see it but youths who are absorbed in fame, diversion, and the thought of the future? But take away diversion, and you will see them dried up with weariness. They feel then their nothingness without knowing it; for it is indeed to be unhappy to be in insufferable sadness as soon as we are reduced to thinking of self, and have no diversion.

Pascal also asserted:

> The only thing which consoles us for our miseries is diversion, and yet this it the greatest of our miseries. For it is this which principally hinders us from reflecting upon ourselves, and which makes us insensibly ruin ourselves. Without this we should be in a state of weariness, and this weariness would spur us to seek a more solid means of escaping from it. But diversion amuses us, and leads us unconsciously to death.

Apathy is merely the attitude, lifestyle, or mindset that states, "I don't care" or "whatever." Like Jimmy Buffett once said, "Is it ignorance or apathy? Hey, I don't know and I don't care." There is no care, no commitments, no conviction, no enthusiasm, and no passion.

Helen Keller claimed, "We may have found a cure for most evils; but we have found no remedy for the worst of them all, the apathy of human beings." But interestingly what we have observed is that liberated students free themselves from the horrific vice of apathy when they were personally impacted by personal pain and suffering. Like C. S. Lewis affirmed, "God whispers to us in our pleasures, speaks in our consciences, but shouts in our pains. It is his megaphone to rouse a deaf world."

"Should I Worry about the Quality of My College/University?"

I (Raul) was fortunate to attend a private university for my undergraduate education. I went as a result of a music/academic scholarship that paid for most of my tuition, so I was very grateful for the opportunity. However, the scholarship didn't extend into the summer months, so I went back home each summer and took courses at the local college. There, I found myself learning in a different way and learning how to think differently as well. In one of my classes on a particular day, in a discussion of "opportunity," one classmate had the view that in order to go to a private school, you had to have a lot of money – so all students who attended private schools were wealthy (theory of reductionism). Rather than speaking up in class, I decided to let that moment pass, because not only was I shy back then (introverted), but I also didn't want to stir the pot or create any conflict (something that I've learned from and has dissipated with time). Interestingly, I had already learned back then what my fellow classmate didn't seem to understand: *It's not where you go to school but what you do with the educational opportunities that you have*. I absorbed and learned so much from my courses at the local college because I adopted the mindset to think past the curriculum and take the time to really listen and learn. Not just learn for the test, but to look at the big picture and apply it to my worldview. You see, professors at different universities often adopt the same materials and references for their classes! If you read to learn and follow the steps in this book, you will essentially learn more than you ever thought you could! It didn't matter that I was taking a full load each summer to complete a double degree and graduate on time with my peers. I decided to be grateful for the experiences I had and make the most of them. It wouldn't have mattered if I had received instruction from a different teacher at a more prestigious university those summers. I was in control of my learning, my exposure to education, and my experiences.

Interestingly, in the same class that particular summer, the midterm was an essay exam. On my test, I cited references in my answers, not because I had been told to do so, but because I wanted to do so for my benefit. After class one day (after grading the exams), my instructor pulled me aside, commended me on my exam, and proceeded to ask me questions about my prior education, namely, what university I currently attended. She assumed that I had to be from a more rigorous university, because I cited my answers on my test. The truth was, I was attending another university, but I hadn't learned to cite my references there! My motivation to become better and do more in class came from my experiences in her class that summer!

> "Try and understand what part you have to play in the world in which you live. There's more to life than you know and it's all happening out there. Discover what part you can play and then go for it."
>
> —Sir Ian Mckellen

CHAPTER ELEVEN

Analyze the Arts

"Through art we can know another's view of the universe."

—MARCEL PROUST

One of the most powerful ways our lives are shaped is through the arts. The films we watch, the music we hear, the stories we read, and even the video games we play cultivate certain desires, inform the mind, redirect personal goals, and help us to envision new possibilities. The lyrics, the beats, and the melodies are not only heard, but they also can be felt. We identify with the rhythms and rhymes, recall particular moments experienced, and re-awaken certain dreams. We walk away from movies that awe-struck us with visual images, moving sounds, and stories that pulled on our emotions, filled our minds, and touched our senses.

Interestingly, gifted actors, movie directors, songwriters, and storytellers are not only creating art, but also advancing, persuading, and impacting us with ideas. In fact, one of the greatest paths or ways to disseminate ideas to an audience is through entertainment (e.g., movies; music). Framed by great stories and personalities, the visuals and the sounds we behold in the privacy of our homes are the most significant classrooms of today. In fact, given our growing indoor lifestyle with technology at our fingertips, the electronic comforts of home (reaching across the world in mere seconds), and our need for connectivity, even physical nature itself is no longer our constant teacher (Don't forget about the lifesaving tip on connecting with nature from chapter 5). In fact, if asked, nature is sometimes perceived as being equated with a nearby park or national forest. But we digress...

> "Art and science... becomes rivals about who owns the truth."
>
> —JACQUES BARZUN

We suspect if you are similar to us, you are likely to think about the entertainment value of the arts. Will the song stir our affections, heal our pain, and delight our senses? Will the arts move us? Make us laugh? Will the movie put us on the edge of our seats? Will we be able to forget our troubles, even if for a couple of hours? But what the arts offer is more than a break, a respite, a pause in our busy lives. Listening to a song can take us back to a memorable moment in time; whether it is positive or negative. Other forms of entertainment have the same power. When we come to love a specific scene, hear a striking or memorable line, see a particular behavior we admire, we will attempt to reflect upon them; the sights, songs, and styles become part of us.

Or consider it a different way...

In our society, we see visual images of physical beauty everywhere. We open the internet, unfold a paper, turn on the TV, pick up a magazine, look up at a billboard, or enter into a clothing store, and we see images of beautiful people who seem to have it all together physically. Cut, defined, and augmented in the right places; unblemished, tanned, and smooth; bright eyes, lustrous hair, and perfect lips; tall, skinny, and proportionally curved. These images surround us as we go about living our lives tackling the difficult, facing the mundane, and hoping for relief from the daily grind of responsibilities. There is hardly a place we can go where these "perfected" images do not bombard us.

Our culture idolizes beauty. To be sure, this is not a recent trend. Human civilization has always prized physical beauty. From Joseph in Egypt to Queen Cleopatra; from Aphrodite to Helen of Troy; From European Queen Eleanor of Aquitaine to Marilyn Monroe; From fictional characters like Wonder Woman and Emma Frost to certain Anime characters such as Yagami from Death Note, Pegasus from Yu-Gi-Oh, Howl the Wizard from Howl's Moving Castle, and video game characters like Ezio Auditore, Master Chief, Zelda, and Laura Croft. People love to be associated with physical beauty. But underneath the images, ideas are being communicated, shaping us in ways we have never considered.

Critically Engage the Arts

While this is only a starting point for analyzing the arts, Dutch art critic Hans Rookmaaker (1922-1977), founder of the art history department at the Free University in Amsterdam, offers a very practical, beneficial four-fold analysis that is applicable to a wide array of the arts we encounter:[41]

Technical Excellence (Formal Analysis)	Integration of Form & Content
Analysis of the Arts	
Thematic Veracity (Intellectual Content)	Honesty (Integrity)

---

[41] Hans Rookmaaker, "Norms for Art and Entertainment" *in The Complete Works of Hans Rookmaaker,* ed. Marleen Hengelaar-Rookmaaker (Pinquet Publishing, 2002), 3:76-9. Also, Jean-Anne Sutherland & Kathryn Feltey, *Cinematic Sociology: Social Life in Film* (Thousand Oaks, CA: Pine Forge Press, 2010), offers a beneficial sociological analysis to evaluating films.

Step 1: Technical Excellence

Analyze the art product in terms of its technical excellence. The greater your observations, the more comprehensive your analysis will be. For example, let's consider films. Evaluate aspects of the film: acting (characterizations), angles, costumes, dialogue, direction (pace), lenses, lighting, plot, production design, set design, shots, special effects, score, and themes.

In order to help you do this critical evaluation well, we recommend that you take humanity and fine art courses that involve teaching you how to understand how art, films, and music are made, what techniques are used, who are the major creators and contributors, and what movements added to, changed, or influenced artistic change and development. Moreover, approach the arts with curiosity. Like reading a book to understand, ask the same questions when beholding an image, listening to a song, watching a movie, or laughing at a sitcom: What do you see? How did they come to that conclusion? The more observations you make, the better your interpretation will likely be.

> "With the most primitive means the artist creates something which the most ingenious and efficient technology will never be able to create."
>
> —KASIMIR MALEVICH

Step 2: The Integration of Form and Content

Analyze the integration of the form and its content. In other words, is the particular form of art sympathetic or appropriate to its meaning? What is the artist's intended message and does it correspond with the specific form of art? For example, consider the popular Christmas hymn, "Silent Night! Holy Night!" The lyrics match the traditional form sung. But if the lyrics were applied to heavy metal music, for example, the integration between the form and content will fail to match, but it would also affect our understanding of the artist's intended meaning. Therefore, ask yourself, how does the form harmonize with the content?

Step 3: Thematic Veracity

Analyze the intellectual content of the art product. Does the art product advance, promote, or state an idea or a truth-claim that corresponds with reality, identifies things as they actually are? In other words, what are the truth-claims being advanced via the arts, both verbal and non-verbal? For example, if the art product proclaims a message that violence is morally in the best interest of personal development and the well-being of society, then we already know that this truth-claim possesses a number of problems (e.g., lack of empirical adequacy; existential relevance; explanatory power). Additionally, within the analysis of this third inquiry, use the following worldview categories from chapter 3 as a guide to analyzing the assumptions, ideas, or truth-claims being made verbally and/or non-verbally:

1   God?

2   Reality?

3   Truth?

4   Knowledge?

5   Humanity?

6   Ethics?

7   Evil?

8   Beauty?

A Closer Look into the Intellectual Content of the Arts

For example, how is the idea of God being advanced? Options could include: (1) There is no God; (2) God is irrelevant; (3) There are multiple independent gods; (4) God is finite, limited; (5) God is an energy force; not a person; (6) We can't know that God exists; (7) God is evil; (8) God is revealed to us in Jesus Christ, the God-man.

Consider reality: (1) Are our surroundings real? (2) Is there more to reality than what we can observe with our five senses? (3) Is reality only a dream?

(4) Does reality possess both physical and spiritual, material and immaterial dimensions? (5) Do we construct reality? (6) Does reality exist apart from us knowing it?

How is "truth" advanced in the arts? For example, (1) Is truth mere opinion? (2) Is truth factual, telling it like it is? (3) Is truth that which a group of people believe at a given time and location? (4) Is truth relative to a particular individual or to a specific culture? (5) There is no truth? (6) Is truth out there? (7) Is truth stranger than fiction?

What about knowledge? For example, arts may advocate the notion that knowledge is acquired from (1) logical reasoning alone (rationalism), (2) five senses alone (empiricism), (3) mysticism or religious encounters, (4) cultic rituals, (5) divine revelation, (6) computer data ports, or (7) intuition.

What are we? Where did we come from? These are questions involving our humanity. The arts may advance the idea that we are (1) nothing more than bio-chemical machines, (2) an accidental byproduct of time, energy, and chance, or (3) a physical and spiritual being created by God.

> "When we contemplate the world of Epicurus, and conceive
> the universe to be a fortuitous jumble of atoms, there is nothing
> grand in this idea. The clashing of atoms by blind chance has nothing
> in it fit to raise our conceptions, or to elevate the mind. But the regular
> structure of a vast system of beings, produced by creating power,
> and governed by the best laws which perfect wisdom and goodness
> could contrive, is a spectacle which elevates the understanding,
> and fills the soul with devout admiration."
>
> —THOMAS REID

Ethics often looms large in the arts since it deals with our conceptions of morality, its foundations, formations, principles, and consequences, individually, the life of the organized community, and collectively as a society.

(1) What is right from wrong? (2) What is good? (3) What is evil? (4) What will benefit society? (5) How will this action benefit others? (6) How do we resolve an ethical dilemma or social problem? (7) Who or what decides what is right and wrong?

What idea about evil is advanced in the arts? (1) Is evil simply ignorance, (2) bad choices, or (3) intolerance? (4) Or is evil something more like the corruption of all things that are good? (5) Is evil a product of civilization? (6) Or is evil simply something we merely distaste? (7) Is evil glamorized as being good or is what is good now considered to be evil?

But merely observing the truth-claims being advanced, disseminated, proclaimed verbally, visually, or physically through the arts, is not enough. We also must look for the justifications of those truth-claims. Here's why. Though we can enjoy the arts immensely, we must understand that the makers of our culture are operating from their own worldviews. The arts can be sources of propaganda, that is, tools to influence, persuade, and even condition a particular audience, a community, and even a nation. If the medium is powerful, then it can persuade the audience to embrace a truth-claim they would not have considered otherwise.

> "Truth will not make us rich, but it will make us free."
>
> —WILL DURANT, THE STORY OF PHILOSOPHY[42]

The Justification of Truth-Claims within the Arts

Are the ideas or truth-claims even validated? What are the justifications? Adapting the following categorical insights from James Sire, a worldview scholar, can help us to understand these principles better. Are the justifications sociological (e.g., community; family; peer-pressure), psychological (e.g., comfort; peace of mind), religious or spiritual (e.g., religious texts; tradition), or philosophical (e.g., coherence; pragmatism)? Are they convincing?[43] If so, how and why?

---

[42] Durant, *The Story of Philosophy*, xxvi.
[43] Carson, *Telling the Truth*, 93, 101.

Sociological:	Psychological:	Religious:	Philosophical:
Culture	Comfort	Authority	Coherence
Family	Hope	(Guru; Imam;	(Harmony)
Friends	Identity	Pastor; Priest;	Completeness
Peer Pressure	Meaning	Rabbi)	(best explanation
	Purpose	Tradition	given all the
	Significance	Religious	evidence)
		Institution	Consistency
		Religious Texts	Workability
		(Scripture)	

"Every good painter paints what he is."

—REMBRANDT

Step 4: Authenticity

Lastly, does the artist, creator, movie director, singer, songwriter, etc. sincerely or authentically believe in the statements within the art form? In other words, does the idea or truth-claim stated, explained, and advanced betray the artist's worldview? To be sure, this fourth analysis may involve studying the background or history of the artist.

"Art tries, literally, to picture the things which philosophy tries to put into carefully thought-out words."

—HANS ROOKMAAKER

Step 5: Harmonize Four Judgments Together

(Apply the test of coherence)

After this four-fold analysis takes place, harmonize all four together. The greater the harmonization between the four judgments (e.g., technical excellence; integration of form and content; thematic veracity; honesty), the more valuable the particular art-product is believed to be. This is evidenced when we reflect upon timeless works of art ranging from architecture to pictures, sculptures to songs, and movies to shows. Beauty, like goodness and truth, can generate social and personal change that will qualitatively enrich ourselves (our own uniqueness), our families, and our communities. Even if not, the coherence method of evaluation is a helpful tool for critical engagement.

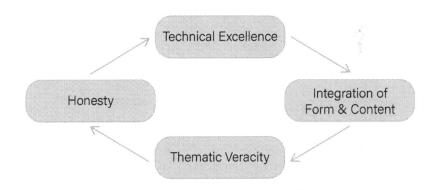

This anti-reductionistic, holistic approach not only takes art products very seriously, but it also considers the ideas being communicated. Ideas can have good or bad consequences. When communicated via the arts, they can be quite powerful in capturing our minds, winning our affections, and shaping our wills. The arts have the power to make an idea so captivating that we want to identify, embrace, and attempt to live it out. Therefore, this analysis demands careful observation, thoughtful engagement, and solid research. Like the relationship between C. S. Lewis and J. R. R. Tolkien, when evaluation takes place within a community where insights can be shared, debated, and defended, iron sharpens iron.

"The essence of beautiful art, all great art, is gratitude."

—FRIEDRICH NIETZSCHE

Conclusion

Evaluating the arts can be a messy project. People can be very disagreeable about what makes great art, whether beauty is subjective or objective, what counts as an aesthetic experience, and whether certain forms of art should be censored. But what we can generally agree upon is this: (1) the arts are generated from within culture; (2) the arts can reflect or mirror culture; (3) the arts can predict where culture is going; (4) the arts can advance personal and social change.

Therefore, it behooves us to take the arts seriously. Why? The arts feed us while we feast on them. There is a dynamic interplay between culture, who and what we behold, and where we are going; the arts affect and infect our being and our becoming. While the arts create moments of connection, a meaningful sense of identity and belonging, generate pleasure, and promote reflection, they can also influence, redirect, and shape us in ways we can easily overlook; the arts can literally be an "opium for the masses," especially in a society that values what is exotic, indulgent, sensational, and sensual, mocks what is healthy, sacred, and wholesome, and neglects the values of the first principles of logic (e.g., Law of Non-Contradiction).

But if we can think about the arts with excellence, using this four-fold approach as a starting point, we can observe, evaluate, reflect, and contribute in a way that goes beyond what we ever thought possible. We will move beyond the temporary escape of laughter and tears, the pleasureable and the painful, the historical and imaginative, the vulgar and the elegant, the kitsch and the beautiful, the protests and self-expression to the desires and demands of the consumers to another realm, namely, critical evaluation and thoughtful contributions. In essence, thinking with excellence about the arts will provide the navigation we need to enjoy the best of what the arts have to offer, create art that qualitatively contributes to society, while not feasting on the arts that are anemic and cheap, engendering empty and costly addictions.

"Addiction, as the psychologists point out, is a function of easy rewards. The addict is someone who presses again and again on the pleasure switch, whose pleasures by-pass thought and judgement to settle in the realm of need. Art is at war with effect addiction, in which the need for stimulation and routinized excitement has blocked the path of beauty by putting acts of desecration centre stage. Why this addiction should be so virulent now is an interesting question: whatever the explanation, my argument implies that the addiction to effect is the enemy not only of art but also of happiness, and that anybody who cares for the future of humanity should study how to revive the 'aesthetic education', as Schiller described it, which has the love of beauty as its goal."

—ROGER SCRUTON, *BEAUTY*[44]

[44] Roger Scruton, *Beauty: A Very Short Introduction* (New York: Oxford University Press, 2009, 2011), 156.

LIFESAVING TIPS

"How Do We Know if Anything Actually Happened in the past?"

This question asked is beneficial in thinking with excellence! Personally indebted to the scholarship of historian Dr. Gary Habermas, we've come to discover that reasonable historians will use at least four sources to determine what has happened in the past. They draw upon apparent memories, the testimony of others either oral or written (e.g., eyewitnesses; primary and secondary documents), and physical traces like archeological discoveries that point to the event in question. This information is harmonized together, and scientific principles are applied. Consider the following principles used.[45]

1   **Early evidence principle:** Early evidence is needed for a case to be well-established.

2   **Eyewitness principle:** Eyewitnesses of that event is preferred.

3   **Multiple independent sources** significantly strengthen the case.

4   Details are enhanced by the **principle of embarrassment, surprise, or negative reports** whereby the writer (who has a friendly vested interested) makes painful remarks concerning an event, person, or even oneself.

5   **Antagonistic principle:** Person or party recognizes the event or person investigated.

6   **Historical coherence principle:** The event coheres with other attested historical events, persons, and situational setting.

---

[45]   Adapted from Gary R. Habermas and Antony G. N. Flew, *Resurrected? An Atheist and Theist Dialogue*, ed. by John F. Ankerberg (Lanham, MD: Rowman and Littlefield, 2005), 1-7; Gary R. Habermas, *Ancient Evidence for the Life of Jesus: Historical Records of His Death and Resurrection* (Nashville: Thomas Nelson, 1984), 124-130.

7   **Scrutinization principle:** Finally, the explanation proposed is scrutinized in order to see if the explanation sheds light on other known phenomena or investigated claims.

If we take these sources and apply these seven scientific principles to them, we have a good starting point for believing something has actually happened in the past. Of course, further inquiries can be made, given future discoveries. These historical skills can be applied to your wide array of tools for navigating the college experience and beyond!

> "It is a good rule after reading a new book, never to allow yourself another new one till you have read an old one in between."
>
> —C. S. Lewis

Questions to Ask Every Educator You Admire

When we visit with educators who we admire, find intriguing, or who are challenging, we should consider asking them the following questions: (1) What books, fiction or non-fiction, have enriched your life the most; (2) What authors do you read the most; (3) What books do you re-read? (4) What is your top 10 list of books or authors every person should read? (5) What is your all-time favorite work?

This not only tells you a lot about what influenced your professor but also can give you direction on which authors or books you should consider reading. Depending upon your field of study, and the people you ask, you might discover certain repeated names, books, patterns, and schools of thought developing in the lists people give; know them! For example, in the field of philosophy of religion, I (Paul) kept seeing names of people like Alvin Plantinga, C. S. Lewis, Richard Swinburne, Eleanor Stump, and Nicholas Wolterstorff. Consequently, I started reading their writings. Do the same in your field of study.

Relatedly, we highly encourage you to read not only the classic works in your field(s) of study but also works that have influenced human civilization. You don't have to read the most significant books immediately, of course. But it should be one of those life-long goals. At the end of each year, I (Paul) like to take some time to read a biography of someone who is not immediately relevant to my research but who made an impact in Western or Eastern civilizations (e.g., Alexander the Great; C. I. Scofield). I have found this personal tradition of reading a biography to be most worthwhile on so many levels.

Know Your Library

"A library is a place where you learn
what teachers were afraid to teach you."

—Alan M. Dershowitz

If you plan to continue your education (i.e., graduate school) then you need to know who are the most prominent and provocative leaders, past and present, in your choice of studies. Who are they? What are their contributions? What works did they produce? Regularly review books, periodicals (journals, magazines, or newspapers that are "routinely" published) and look for names, ideas, resources, and patterns that keep emerging. Take time to look at the new books purchased by your school library or local bookstore that are put on display. What are they? Who wrote them?

While attending Dallas Theological Seminary, I (Paul) would visit the periodical section of the library about every three weeks. In the periodical section are collections of journals, magazines, newsletters, and newspapers that are regularly published. Some of them are published:

1   Weekly (every week)

2   Midweekly (middle of the week)

3   Bimonthly or semimonthly (twice a month)

4   Monthly (once a month)

5   Quarterly (every three months)

6   Annually (once a year)

7   Biannually or semiannually (twice a year)

8   Biennial (every two years)

9   Triennial (every third year)

10 Aperiodic or nonperiodic (no regular interval).

I would look at the journal titles, authors, themes, and abstracts. If there were articles that I thought would benefit me in some way, whether immediately or years from now, I would copy each of them, staple the pages together, and place them all in my file cabinet. It didn't take much time at all to discover who were the "movers and shakers" in contemporary fields of study and what classic, critical, or novel works they engaged, critiqued, or used to support their own views. This information would lead me to consider knowing who those authors were, what works they produced, and what consequences (potential or actual) flowed from their ideas or studies.

After much time these periodicals would be bound into a volume and placed into "stacks" which are library shelving space or even some type of storage area. Periodicals and certain books can be placed into "open stacks" or "closed stacks." These stacks, whether open or closed, may be found in the "periodical" section of the library. "Open stacks" are bookshelves available for people to browse whereas "closed stacks" are those areas only accessible to library staff; they will retrieve whatever you need.

By knowing my library, studying the periodicals, and looking at new books put on display, I discovered that I was able to engage in a wide array of issues that even transcended my particular fields of study. To be sure, this paid dividends when I was interviewed for a faculty position when two other prospective faculty members were being considered.

Many libraries are moving their periodicals online, which offers easier access from the comforts of places such as our homes, allowing us to save time from hunting down and perhaps copying what we need. However, there is something adventurous, kinesthetic, and aesthetically pleasing about touching books, turning pages, and discovering other articles, authors, and books we may have never even considered; we may be surprised by what we find!

Learning is pleasurable. Every time we walk into a library, we always get more than what we originally planned! Support your library. Librarians not only help to preserve the past, but they help preserve the future. Moreover, like a good gym promotes cardiovascular health, muscular development, and wellbeing, a good library enlightens the mind, engenders creativity, and challenges you to grow and think critically.

"Libraries store the energy that fuels the imagination.
They open up windows to the world and inspire us to explore
and achieve, and contribute to improving our quality of life.
Libraries change lives for the better."

—SIDNEY SHELDON

CHAPTER TWELVE

The Limits of Education

"If our condition were truly happy we should not need
to divert ourselves from thinking about it."

—Blaise Pascal

The day finally arrived! My (Paul) life-long dream was about to be realized! After countless hours of reading, assignments, research projects, classroom instruction, and conversations with students and professors from three other institutions, I was about to finally graduate with my Ph.D. in philosophy from Texas A&M University. This was my fourth and last degree. But an interesting thing happened to me the day after I walked the graduation stage, enjoyed festivities with friends and family, and whole heartedly expressed appreciation to those who supported me all these years. The next morning, I realized all my insecurities remained. Even after reaching this long-term goal, all my own baggage, frailties, and propensities remained.

I (Raul) had a similar experience with lingering insecurities after completing my degrees. I realized that despite my educational accomplishments, a promising offer to teach at a stellar institution, and support from my family, uncertainty remained. Particularly, there was the realization of a void, along with an urge to take a mental break. You see, my educational experiences challenged me and pushed me to strive for excellence. However, much like people adjust after life changes, I soon realized that I was heading towards a period of adjustment as well: life after educational pursuits. And despite the fact that I would continue in the field of education and continue learning (professor at the university level), I still experienced a feeling of loss, much like the death of a loved one. Interestingly, I also realized that there were parts of me that had been neglected as I completed my education. I knew in the back of my mind that I needed more learning, that I needed to pursue more knowledge to become the type of person and professor that I wanted to be.

The Limits of Education

What happens when our longings and needs are not fulfilled by education, when emptiness still follows us even after our goals are achieved, when we discover the pleasures of education did not fill the void within, heal our "baggage," or make us whole?

First, enjoy but do not live for education. In other words, be nourished by education but don't allow it to become an idol in your life. Some of us think that if I only go to this school, sit under this professor, receive this award, write this book, and speak around the world that it will be the remedy to our existential situation. But what we discover is no matter how many degrees we obtain, the accolades received by peers, and the positions earned, the deep struggles within, the search for significance, meaning, identity, and fulfillment remain.

Therefore, education is not the answer to fill that void. To be sure, education nourishes us, enlarges our vision of the world and our relationship to it, enables us to make connections that would not otherwise have been seen, and gives us practical skills to navigate through the oscillating moments of stability and instability in living life, and engenders surprising and rich relationships with people that can last a lifetime. Education enables us to connect the past with our present circumstances to generate a better future for our posterity. Moreover, ideas have consequences. Some ideas have good consequences, and other ones have bad consequences. Thus, a good education helps us engage and stand firm for the particular freedoms and values we enjoy against ideas, personalities, and movements who seek to wreak havoc on what is true, good, and beautiful (e.g., Nazism; racial discrimination; homophobia; religious persecution).

And remember, a good education comes from within. There is a famous meme where someone has found happiness and a second person approaches them and asks, "Where did you find that?" The person who found happiness says, "I created it myself." We create our own happiness, and we make the most out of our own education and our lives.

> "The cultivated mind is the guardian genius of democracy."
>
> —Mirabeau Lamar

Second, counterfeit or pseudo-solutions are not the answer to our human dilemma. When we discover that education does not fill the void, many of us turn to the alluring and crafty pseudo-solutions or counterfeit answers like diversions, indifference, money, and sex and violence. [46]

Counterfeit Solution # 1: Trivial Diversions

Don't try to find the solution of happiness in trivial diversions in such areas as adventuring, entertainment, gaming, material objects, popularity, power, sex, and wealth. They will only magnify the problem if not lead you to places you never thought you would go, extracting the best parts of your person-hood *and more*. Not only will your restlessness remain, but it will also be compounded by anger, brokenness, and even depression.

---

[46] Kreeft, *Christianity for Modern Pagans*, 167-206.

Counterfeit Solution # 2: Apathy

Don't also try to dull the pain by indifference. Apathy, as evidenced in statements like "anything goes," "live and let live," "you do your own thing, and I do my own thing," and "whatever," is not the answer. In fact, the mindset of apathy will only make the situation worse. Consider the words of philosophers Dr. Peter Kreeft of Boston College and Blaise Pascal:

> "But the only long-range solution to pain, whether physical or spiritual,
> is to listen to what it is telling us. It is a symptom. We must follow its
> clue, like a river, or a guide through the jungle, if we want to be healed.
> Perpetual difference is like shutting off the alarm clock and going back
> to sleep when the house you are in, which you have built on the sand,
> is about to be washed away into the sea."[47]

—Dr. Peter Kreeft

> "Those who do not love truth excuse themselves on the grounds
> that it is disputed and that very many people deny it.
> Thus, the error is solely due to the fact that they love neither
> true nor charity, and so they have no excuse."

—Blaise Pascal

While we are on the subject of mindset and apathy, it is important to mention that we are in control of how we view ourselves, our abilities, our limitations, and our perseverance. Dr. Carol Dweck in her book *Mindset*[48] discusses the idea that there are two default mindsets that each person may possess: the fixed mindset and the growth mindset. People with a fixed

---

[47] *Ibid.*, 189.
[48] See Carol S. Dweck, *Mindset: The New Psychology of Success* (New York: Ballantine Books, 2008).

mindset tend to be apathetic, they accept their limitations and liken them to who they are. Fixed mindset individuals will fail at a task and make the claim that it's because they are not good at that particular task. In contrast, people with the growth mindset look at failure as a challenge. Growth mindset individuals will fail at a task and make the claim that they have to try harder next time and learn from their failures. It's the idea that they are not good at a particular task – yet. They do not accept their limitations but, instead, learn from them and grow to overcome them. Be a growth mindset person!

> "The chief cause of failure and unhappiness is trading what you want most for what you want right now."
>
> —Zig Ziglar

Counterfeit Solution # 3: Sex and Violence

While some people attempt to fill this void with trivial diversions (e.g., material things, things, and more things), others to turn to apathy (which poisons everything it touches), and, still, others turn to sex and violence. This emptiness goes beyond projecting an "imaginary" life before others, hoping that by convincing them we convince ourselves that we are more than what we actually are. Instead, we give into the debasing idea that if we are unhappy, then others should be too! So, we exploit others, dehumanizing them through empty sex and violence whereby people are not viewed as people possessing inherent value with their own set of dreams, gifts, and freedoms, but physical objects to abuse, damage, and hurt. Coupled with jealousy, we destroy what blessings they received, the goods they earned, and the accomplishments they achieved.

What is the answer for a life of satisfaction if it is not education, diversions like material objects, the application of indifference to life, or the destruction of people's lives and possessions via sex and violence?

I (Raul) have three teenage boys and one teenage girl. In our home, we have very authentic conversations about how to find happiness and also how to treat others. Whenever my children talk about friends or potential "more than friends" situations, I always remind them of something that an acquaintance once told me. When you are interacting with a potential love interest, remember they are likely someone's future spouse (unless it's true love between the two of you) and your future spouse is likely out there somewhere as well. How would you want another person to treat your future spouse? Likewise, the person you are seeing also may become a future spouse to someone else. Treat them with the utmost respect and honor. My children at this point know the entire spiel as I deliver it. But, to me, the message is so important and so needed in today's world. And, I always end my conversations with them by reminding them to respect themselves.

Think With Excellence!

Instead of turning to counterfeit or pseud-solutions to find happiness, use the skills you have gained from *Thinking with Excellence*, and take the search on for yourself. How?

First Step: Examine Your Worldview Assumptions

Let's return to your own eight worldview assumptions about the following:

1   Your view of **God**

2   Your view of **Reality**

3   Your view of **Truth**

4   Your view of **Knowledge**

5   Your view of **Humanity**

6   Your view of **Ethics**

7   Your view of **Evil**

8   Your view of **Beauty**

Before you pursue and sort out the truth-claims regarding the fulfillment of our existential longings, it is critical to examine those eight assumptions of your own worldview.

Ask yourself which assumptions possess the greatest logical force (logical consistency) and empirical evidences, are the most existentially relevant, workable and viable, and engender moral and aesthetic excellence. What is your justification? In other words, what and why do you believe what you believe? Are your beliefs supported by facts? Impressions? Opinions? Your eight assumptions will possess structural integrity to handle the weighty problems, changes, and even the problems we create within ourselves if they are supported by facts, not mere impressions or opinions, that possess the greatest explanatory power, relevance, and workability.

Second Step: The Strength of Your Worldview

The strength of your worldview is not only dependent upon the eight individual components, but also how they harmonize or cohere together. This is testing your worldview through what we learned earlier in *Thinking with Excellence*, namely, coherence:

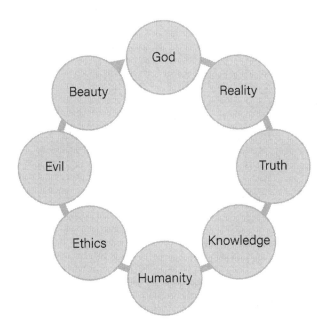

The greater the harmony between these eight assumptions and the evidences that support each one, the stronger your worldview will be. But coherence as a test alone is insufficient. These eightfold assumptions need to match or harmonize with reality as it actually is as its foundation, all governed by facts. The greater the actual testability of those beliefs with reality as it is, the stronger the worldview will likely be.

Third Step: What Do You Live for?

Given the vaporous conditions of our lives, that is, we are here for a moment in time and gone the next like steam from a hot cup of coffee, what is truly worth living for? This question will help clarify what is most important. Once again, education will not generate ultimate meaning, purpose, and significance or fill the incompleteness within. Sort out what is valuable in your life from what is not. Then ask yourself what occupies your life the most? Are you spending most of your energy, resources, and time on what is trivial or important, beneficial or dangerous? In other words, are you giving your "leftovers" to what matters most?

> "The biggest human temptation is to settle for too little."
>
> —THOMAS MERTON

Fourth Step: Be Open-Minded

Be open-minded and, therefore, a lover of truth. Be open to truth-claims, even those that may be foreign to your personal experience. Don't be close-minded, even if you are hurting, your own dreams are never realized, or if something you have loved has been taken from you. Moreover, do not allow your feelings to immobilize you. Allow those painful experiences to enable you to find the answers to the ultimate questions of life.

Fifth Step: Know the Ultimate Questions

Taking into account your worldview and those from whose answers you will be considering, here are some of the most ultimate questions of life:

- Where do we come from? (origin)

- What are we? Who are we? (Identity)

- Why are we here? (meaning)

- How should we live? (morality)

- What's gone wrong with the world? (evil)

- What can be done to fix the problems of the world? (hope)

- What is the good life? (happiness)

Sixth Step: Use the Sevenfold Approach to Evaluate Answers

Think with excellence using the critical skills of analysis you have learned in this work to engage the given from all sorts of people making contradictory answers. This noisy clamor of everyone telling you what you should embrace can be quite mind numbing, deafening, and exhausting. But by applying what you have learned in *Thinking with Excellence* you can sort out which worldviews best answers those ultimate questions:

1   Which answer is most logically consistent?

2   Which answer provides the most considerable amount of evidences?

3   Which answer is most relevant, germane, and relatable to these struggles of the human condition?

4   Which answer is most workable? How does it "cash" out in day-to-day living? If something is true, then it will work while what works may not necessarily be true.

5   Which answer is most viable or worthwhile to embrace?

6   Which answer provides the greatest explanatory power, pulling together all of life, and even shedding light on other inquiries?

7   Which answer engenders or promotes virtue (moral habits of excellence), affirms moral and aesthetic values, duties, and accountability we collectively share and enriches and honors our lives personally and the communities in which we are embedded?

Seventh Step: Learn from the Past

Never neglect history. While history offers a vast record of persons, positions, and perspectives, realize that many of the questions and answers given have already been raised by some of the most gifted thinkers and institutions in the history of thought and culture. While the authority of antiquity or the authority of what is new, novel, and popular is not a legitimate justification for any position, we do a disservice to ourselves when we forgo investigating not only their answers, but also how they even raise the questions we are considering. Moreover, the historical and cultural context in which these questions and answers emerge may shed incredible light into our own inquiries in ways we have never pondered.

In fact, when we examine our history and connect it to the present, we can reduce the cacophony or dissonant voices into at least three major options:

Door # 1: There are no ultimate answers. We live in a universe that is ultimately meaningless because we are the accidental product of time, energy, and chance. Thus, in the end, whatever we do, whether good or bad, it doesn't ultimately matter for there is no purpose to our accidental emergence from nothingness. There is no God. Consequently, Albert Camus, an atheistic existentialist, observed that our lives can be likened to the Greek myth of Sisyphus who was eternally condemned by the gods to push a heavy ball up a slope, only to kick it back down. There is no ultimate purpose, no ultimate destiny, no ultimate accountability or justice, and no ultimate meaning. In a sense, we are on the train of nothingness ultimately going nowhere.

When we die, we die. Knowing our lives are ultimately meaningless, the best we can do is value our freedom, the moment-by-moment choices we make, and take ownership of consequences that follow from what we do and don't do.

"Man is condemned to be free; because once thrown into the world,
he is responsible for everything he does."

—Jean-Paul Sartre

While there is no purpose to the "accident" of human existence, we have to be careful. Even though we are ultimately responsible for the choices we make, the values we embrace, and even the pleasures we pursue in this meaningless, indifferent universe, we can experience these punctuated moments of happiness such as the "aha" moments that take your breath away when you encounter or create a beautiful work of art, commit yourself to alleviating the suffering of others, build a healthy marriage and family, or adopt worthwhile projects that qualitatively nourishes our culture.

> "The meaning of life is not to be discovered only after death
> in some hidden, mysterious realm; on the contrary, it can be found
> by eating the succulent fruit of the Tree of Life and by living in the
> here and now as fully and creatively as we can."
>
> —PAUL KURTZ

Door # 2: We create our own answers. Through such tools as the sciences and/or the arts we can attempt to create answers to the ultimate questions of life. In other words, we are the starting point for not only the way we frame final questions but also how we answer them. While human progress will be central to the pursuit of those answers, we are ultimately responsible for the consequences that flow from those judgments, the lives we affect, the condition and qualities of our communities, and the legacies we leave behind. Thus, we are able to create better people and better societies. Whether God exists or not, he is irrelevant to our iniquities, our endeavors, our possibilities, and our sufferings.

Door # 3: God is the best answer to our ultimate questions. God is the only one who can infinitely give us the happiness, peace, and significance we long to experience. Apart from God, who is absolutely and inseparably good, true, and beautiful, there is no other remedy for our manifold incompleteness. Human solutions are finite and ultimately vacuous. This was the conclusion made by people like C. S. Lewis, the famous Oxford scholar and author. After his conversion to Theism and Christianity following his overriding biographical search for joy, C. S. Lewis observed, "If we find ourselves with a desire that nothing in this world can satisfy, the most probable explanation is that we were made for another world." God Himself can fill this multifaceted void if we turn to Him. Therefore, enjoy the things you have but intimately pursue God; He is available, present, and sufficient.

> "If we don't know that there is such a person as God, we don't know
> the first thing (the most important thing) about each other, our world,
> and ourselves. This is because the most important truths about them,
> and us are that we have been created by the Lord, and utterly depend
> upon him for our continued existence."
>
> —Alvin Plantinga

Conclusion

Applying the skills from *Thinking with Excellence* will give you the resources needed for you and others to evaluate the answers given to life's ultimate questions. Not only will you be able to resist mesmerizing personalities, attractive options, illogical truth-claims, and vices like impatience but you will also not find yourself entrapped by counterfeit or pseudo-solutions like trivial diversions, apathy, sex, and violence. Instead, you will be set apart as a force to be reckoned with against the comfortable ways of living found in the rutted roads of mediocrity, legitimately critique authorities in the marketplace of ideas with civility, be an authentic hero someone can believe in, and make a life-giving difference that will enable you to leave a lasting legacy worth having.

> "It's a dangerous business, Frodo, going out your door.
> You step onto the road, and if you don't keep your feet,
> there's no knowing where you might be swept off to."
>
> —J. R. R. Tolkien, Fellowship of the Ring

LIFESAVING TIPS

"Should I Go to Grad School?"

To decide whether or not you should pursue graduate school, first, determine what profession you are interested in. Sometimes you may not know for sure until after your bachelor's degree, and that is okay. Some individuals like to take a year off between school to gain professional experience while others want to go straight through and finish school without any interruptions. The decision is entirely yours, and there is no right answer. Some things to consider should you decide to pursue graduate school:

1   **GPA is important.** Your GPA, or Grade Point Average, is vital to prospective graduate schools and programs of study. Maintaining a healthy GPA will require you to stay on top of your studies. Most graduate schools rely on GPA averages from undergraduate programs to "weed out" potential students. That being said, can you still get into grad school with a lower GPA? Yes and no. It entirely depends on the requirements of each program.

2   **Experience outside the classroom is critical.** The more opportunities you can obtain during your undergraduate program, the better. Graduate school, while competitive, is still achievable. However, it is imperative to seek out those opportunities to shadow a professional and gain experience outside of the classroom.

3   **Form good relationships with your professors.** Most graduate programs require letters of recommendation (letters of rec). Your classroom professors often provide these letters on your behalf. While letters from employers are acceptable to most programs, many grad schools require letters of rec from faculty with advanced degrees. The rationale for this is that professors often can discuss a student's intellectual abilities and potential for graduate school. Make sure you formally ask a professor and provide them with at least two months to write a letter of recommendation. Be mindful of application deadlines!

4 **Building a resume is required.** Just as most places of employment require a work resume, graduate programs require a "school" resume. The school resume is very similar to a job resume, and you want to include several pieces of information, including prior education, overall GPA, and education opportunities (e.g., work-study; research with professors; honors projects). Moreover, academic resumes should include extracurricular opportunities and anything else salient or worthy for the program to know (e.g., shadowing opportunities; work experience related to the field).

5 **Prepare for the GRE.** The Graduate Record Exam, or GRE, often is a requirement for entrance to a graduate program of study. Do you remember taking the SAT or the ACT to get into college? Well, the GRE is the equivalent to get into grad school. Not all programs require the GRE, therefore, it is critical to check the requirements of your program of interest.

Interested in Grad School? Check out the requirements for graduate programs by visiting school websites and learning of any prerequisites that may be required for study. It is necessary to start early! If you are thinking about going to graduate school immediately after finishing your bachelor's degree, you will want to begin exploring at least one year BEFORE you finish college! The early bird gets the worm!

"You have to find something that you love enough to be able to take risks, jump over hurdles and break through the brick walls that are always going to be placed in front of you. If you don't have that kind of feeling for what it is you are doing, you'll stop at the first giant hurdle."

—GEORGE LUCAS

ANCHOR YOURSELF IN LEARNING

What is the Major Difference Between a College and a University?

In the United States you will discover that educators, students, and institutions will often use the terms "college" and "university" interchangeably. Historically a "college" offers degrees in (a) specific area(s) (e.g., The College of Biblical Studies-Houston) whereas a university (e.g., Stephen F. Austin State University) is composed of a collection of colleges (e.g., Business College; Education; Fine Arts; Forest & Agriculture; Liberal & Applied Arts; Sciences & Math) offering a wide array of programs and degrees. Interestingly, some colleges are universities that retain the name of "college" for sake of tradition (e.g., Boston College). Also, people will use "college" to describe vocational schools that offer a particular skill or trade (e.g., automative technician). In sum, a college will offer degrees in a few areas of study whereas a university is larger in scope with multiple colleges and degrees.

What Is A Priori vs. A Posteriori?

Popularized by Immanuel Kant (1724-1804), two types of knowledge are briefly mentioned at the end of the last chapter:

A priori: Knowledge independent of experience (Latin: *a priori* means "from what is before");

A posteriori: Knowledge dependent on experience (Latin: "from what is after").

What Is Convocation?

Convocation is a large formal assembly of people. At least once a year a college or university will call the students together for a formal gathering. Convocation could be university-wide, college, division, or departmental major wide. You will usually see announcements for convocation every fall semester.

What Is Credit And Debt? Should I Open a Credit Card?

Prof! I am receiving letters from companies about opening credit cards and also from some of my favorite retail stores about in-store credit. What do I do about applying for credit and what is debt?

First, let's start by defining important terms:

Credit – This is a specified amount of money that you are allowed to borrow. Credit cards allow you to borrow money very easily and companies profit off of customers who borrow money over time.

Debt – This is a specified amount of money that you owe. When you borrow money (credit) you ultimately owe it back... with interest.

For example, let's say that you have a credit card with a $1,000 credit limit. Sounds great, doesn't it? And let's say that you get a great deal on a top-of-the-line, wide-screen TV for $500. You may think that you will only pay 500 for that item, however, that depends on how quickly you pay the credit card company back. Your initial debt is $500 but interest accrues over time and you may end up paying closer to $600 or $800 in the end if you don't pay it off quick enough. That's how credit card companies make their money. They bet on the fact that you will delay paying off your purchase. Bottom line: Be very careful with credit cards! You can easily go into debt very quickly if you become an eager spender. Our advice: only borrow what you can pay back quickly!

What's A GPA?

A GPA is an acronym for "Grade Point Average." At the end of every semester you will receive a GPA that is a calculated average of all the final grades you have earned each and every semester. The average is based on 0 to 4.0 or 5.0 scale. You will also have an overall GPA average given at the end of each semester of all the grades earned. When you graduate from college, you will receive a final GPA. If you pursue graduate or professional studies, those institutions will require your final GPA for your undergraduate studies. They will likely have a minimal GPA score earned to even apply to a graduate or professional program. But each college, university, or professional program may differ on what that minimum score earned may be.

Lastly, maintaining a certain GPA is necessary for specific scholarships (to receive and maintain them). Therefore, pay attention to your GPA score, especially if you are planning to further your education, gain entry into a specialized field like nursing, or if you are on a scholarship that demands a minimum GPA.

What Are Loans?

Loans are a monetary amount provided to an individual that must be repaid with interest (an additional amount of money you pay as extra for borrowing money in the first place). There are both private and federal types of student loans, which usually are awarded based on need and also generally have lower interest rates. Private loans are generally from independent lending agencies and have specific credit requirements. In many cases, students can get private loans with their parents or guardians as co-borrowers. Federal loans include programs such as the Stafford Loan, Perkins Loan, and the PLUS loan. These are all through the federal government, based on financial need, and have lower interest rates and flexible repayment plans. To determine if you qualify for a need-based loan, you must fill out a Free Application for Federal Student Aid, or FAFSA. All of the information you need can be found on the federal government website: *www.studentaid. ed.gov.*

What Is Plagiarism?

Plagiarism is the intentional or even unintentional use of someone else's ideas, words, and works without proper attribution, citation, or credit. The word literally comes from a Latin word that means "kidnapper." Thus, plagiarism is a type of stealing. While each college and university may differ in their policies regarding plagiarism, the consequences can be so severe that you will never be able to achieve your academic goals and dreams. Not only is it quite embarrassing to be caught plagiarizing, but you are actually diminishing the rich education you could earn to become all that you might possibly be. Avoid plagiarism at all costs! Moreover, if you gain a reputation for plagiarism, your fellow students or professors may not recommend or help you gain employment or assist you in securing entrance into graduate or professional programs. Given our advanced technology, most colleges and universities now have software programs that are able to detect plagiarism. Our recommendations: (1) Always cite your sources. When in doubt, cite. (2) Ask your professor for resources for proper citation. (3) Many colleges and universities have a style guide for writing. (4) Visit with your professor if you do not understand what you are learning; it is your responsibility to see your professor if you are struggling. (5) Never wait until the last minute to do an assignment, discussion post, group project, or presentation (hence, know your syllabus; look for announcements; practice time management). Most violators commit plagiarism because they waited too late, forgot about a particular requirement, or were not interested in the topic. (6) Don't use the same paper for two or more different classes (this will likely be considered self-plagiarism). (7) Be careful if you share your work with others; they may plagiarize your material. (8) Lastly, it is your responsibility to know what counts as plagiarism and what doesn't. It is never the professor's fault if you commit plagiarism.

What Is Rationalism vs. Empiricism?

Rationalism: Look to logical reason instead of empirical data for origin and justification of beliefs. When knowledge is derived from reason, acquired independently of or prior to sense experience we call this *"a priori* knowledge." For example, 1 + 1 = 2 is *a priori* knowledge. Another example would be "All bachelors are unmarried." (Parmenides; Descartes; Spinoza; Leibniz).

Empiricism: Our source of knowledge comes from the experience of one or more of the 5 senses. When knowledge depends entirely on sense experience, we call this *a posteriori* knowledge. For example, the dog is barking; the cat is on the mat, and Deborah drew a triangle (Heraclitus; John Locke; David Hume).

What Does STEM Mean?

STEM is an acronym or abbreviation that refers to science, technology, engineering, and mathematics. Though they are historically related to a liberal arts education, they are now often seen to be distinguishable from it.

What Is a Study or Travel Abroad?

One of the most enriching aspects of thinking with excellence is cross-cultural experiences. Experiencing a foreign country can enlarge our vision, expand our understanding, and even inform who we are. Study or travel abroad programs are found at most college and universities whereby they facilitate, often between universities, opportunities to travel internationally and study. It is critical to apply early, discover what resources are available (if any), and what options (countries; universities) are available that best advance your personal development, education, and goals. You will also discover that many faculty members are involved in these programs, lecturing and providing oversight over the program that the college or university has created. The programs may last a few weeks, a summer, or even a whole semester or longer. Apply early!

What Is a Syllabus?

A syllabus (syllabi for plural) is a guide to any course of study; it shows you how the particular course is organized. Therefore, on the first day of class (perhaps earlier or even later that first week of school) you will receive a syllabus. The syllabus will typically include the following: professor contact information, class topics, course objectives, office hours of professor, policies, expectations, required and/or recommended texts, class topics, and schedule of assignments. The professor can treat the syllabus as a type of contract between both of you. Therefore, you must not only read the syllabus carefully, but you also must refer back to it repeatedly (every week) to know what material to read, when assignments are due, how to fulfill course objectives, and what rules to follow. To be sure, each professor can be different in what they emphasize and require. So, don't expect each syllabus to be the same, especially given expectations they have for you.

Before you contact the professor about assignments, due dates, or required reading, check your syllabus first.

What Is Work-Study?

Work-study is an opportunity to work on campus. It is a job that is designed to be flexible (part-time) so that students can not only work and receive income and help pay education expenses but also complete their studies at the same time. Several departments offer work-study opportunities for students, and some programs are need-based, which means students must qualify based on financial aid programs. You can check with your school's financial aid office, and they will be able to help you. Depending on the program and availability, some work-study programs are also found off campus. Many of the jobs can be related to your field of study, which provides you with valuable experience in your major area.

"Challenge yourself; it's the only path which leads to growth."

—Morgan Freeman

ADVICE FROM GRADUATE STUDENTS

"The most important lessons I learned in college
were far from what was taught in the classroom."

—Taylor Wilson

"Even the best students will have trouble making it to an 8am class.
Try to schedule classes after 8am!"

—Nikki Thomas

"Failure is an event. You are not a failure if you mess up
or make mistakes."

—Jordan Magruder

"Do what you love and do it often."

—Hannah Kincaid

"Learn to focus on the bigger picture, one test/grade
doesn't define what you can do."

—Sarah Salom

"College isn't a sprint, it's a marathon."

—Kay Mesecher

"Don't get so caught up in your studies that you lose joy
in the little things."

—TAYLOR JOHNSTON

"Learn to prioritize studying time for each class...
and figure out which studying method works best for you!"

—NIKKI BATAGOWER

"Making friends in class makes class easier and more enjoyable."

—HANNAH FULLER

"Make time to eat healthy and stay active.
It helps with a positive mindset."

—KATIE WALKER

"Don't let other people's stress become your stress."

—JULIA TOMLINSON

"Building community may take time and effort,
but those people help define your experience."

—LAYNE SCULL

"Don't be afraid to ask for help from peers/professors."

—RACHEL COLE

"Join groups and organizations to meet people with similar interests."

—HEATHER BURKHALTER

"Don't feel bad for being an undecided major,
career counselors are on campus to help!"

—RACHEL ALLEN

"A good roommate makes all the difference in the world –
be mindful of living situations and make changes if needed."

—STEPHANIE POWELL

"Perfection isn't always key!"

—RAEANNA HUFFMAN

"Always take care of and make time for you because your health
and happiness are a huge part of your success."

—KALEE OWENS

"Don't simply study for the sake of studying... learn how to study!"

—KRISTINA KENNY

"The classroom is a transformative cocoon. Savor the metamorphosis
of growth and you will find the adventure exceedingly more enjoyable.
Study with the aim to grow, not just to get the grade."

—CASEY B. CROCKER

STORIES FROM COLLEGE STUDENTS

The following stories are from undergraduate and graduate students currently enrolled in college. These anonymous stories shed some additional light on the college and university experience and hopefully will provide additional guidance in unexpected ways.

"During my sophomore year of college, I lost my best friend to her battle with cystic fibrosis. We both wanted to be speech pathologists. One of the last things she told me was that she believed in me and that I had to make it for both of us. So I made that my drive and use it every day."

"This semester I found out that I have a thyroid problem. Even though this will affect my life forever, it will not stop me from enjoying my college experience."

"I play softball and have done so since my freshman year. I wanted to be successful both on and off the field. I was hanging around a group I shouldn't have, and one day it just clicked. I realized I wanted to be a better person and player. So I got organized, changed my priorities and focused on the good in life. I've been told 'the game knows who's been putting in the work.' I'm a firm believer that life knows, too."

"I'm a first-generation college student, and a life-changing event in college was when I was accepted into a college program for first-generation students. The program gave me a chance to meet others who are in the same position as I am. It gave me a chance to make friends before I started my first day at school. They helped me adjust to the college life. I will forever be grateful to them."

"My best college experience that changed my life was meeting my roommate and gaining a new best friend. I was absolutely terrified of sharing a space with someone but she turned out to be amazing, and I now have a life-long friend."

"One thing that impacted my college career was getting put on academic probation my freshman year. I didn't tell anyone but my friends because I knew my parents would not be pleased. I had to buckle down and get my head on straight in order to be successful. I would think though – that was the best/worst thing that could have ever happened to me."

"After having three children, I wanted to be sure that they could have a parent with a college education, which is something I did not have. I wanted to be able to teach them about college, so they don't wait as long as I did to get their degree."

"Last semester, a friend of mine at school passed away suddenly in her sleep. For some reason, I never thought that death would be something that impacted my college experience but it did, and it made me realize that you can't take anything or anyone for granted, because today may be all there is."

"Honestly, my biggest life change in college has been learning to be very independent away from my parents/family because we're all very close. So that was extremely hard for me. At the same time, it made me who I am today, and I'm super thankful for that."

"Being a first-generation college student motivated me to do my very best in everything I did. It was extremely difficult but getting help from teachers and friends helped me through it."

"The passing of my grandpa is what has made me change my outlook on college. I now have more of a want to, a reason to succeed...to graduate college and make him proud."

"During my second year, I switched majors because I found myself struggling and making bad grades in my first major area of study. It seemed like I was trying twice as hard as my peers yet still making worse grades than others. It was difficult for me to switch, but I found my second major worked better for me and I finally found myself making As and thriving instead of just getting by."

"I met a group of girls at a church hangout I went to (I didn't want to go) and went to their house the next night, and then went to their church the next Sunday. Me saying yes to an encounter I probably wouldn't have in high school introduced me to my greatest friends and amazing church family."

"I started my college experience at a university in my hometown and lived at home. The best things I ever did for myself was step out of my comfort zone and spontaneously transfer to a university away from home. So many wonderful things have happened because I faced my fears and moved away from home."

"I once failed a test in my history class because I wasn't sure of directions and was afraid to ask in the moment. Now I ask as many questions as I need to, no matter how simple it may seem."

"The best thing about my college experience has been being a part of a college ministry. The people I have met have been so supportive and have really encouraged me and helped me through this season of my life."

"A life-changing thing for me in college was joining the sorority I am in. It allowed me to get involved on campus and meet my best friends. Even if it's not joining a sorority, joining a club or other organization will make your college experience so much better. It teaches you lessons, helps you gain different experiences, and helps you meet amazing people."

"My brother passed away during the spring semester of my freshman year. It was an incredibly hard time, but I held my head up high and finished the semester. I talked to my professors about what happened, and they were very generous to me. I passed all my classes, but it was definitely the hardest thing I've ever had to go through. And it has impacted my college career in many ways."

"I was in a car accident junior year. I lost all my textbooks (they were crushed in my car). I had to miss school because of the surgery I had to have, I had to miss work, etc. Although it was tough, it made me grateful to be alive, made me rely on others and made me work extra hard. Looking back, I am thankful for learning something from it."

"When I came to college I was so broken. I could have easily gone off the deep end, but I found a group of people who loved me in my brokenness and did not let me stay that way. Find your people who love you no matter what and want the best for you."

"I went through a really rough time during my undergrad, changing my major and going through an abusive relationship. I went through a terrible depression and almost dropped out of school. I went to counseling my second year of college and would not have made it through without their help. I kept going about a year after I graduated and they have made such an impact in my life. Please seek help, there is a solution I promise."

"Something I learned while in school is to reach out to the people that are sitting alone or have no friends. You never know what they are going through and you could be a really great friend to them."

"During my last semester of college, my dad had a triple bypass. I learned that, at the end of the day, even though school is extremely important, it's not everything. I had to learn that it is okay to take a step back."

"Never decline an invitation to pursue research with your professor. Once my professor brought a drone to class, exclaiming he needed a volunteer pilot to conduct research. I was the only one who raised a hand. This singular opportunity opened doors I never anticipated. It helped me come to love my major, stand out as an undergraduate student, generate multiple publications with my name on it, and create job opportunities that others did not receive. It even led to a job for my younger brother. Finally, by volunteering that one day a genuine mentorship was created with my professor that pays dividends even today."

"It wasn't until I was done with college that I realized that college is for you! You are the project for the next four years. Don't let anyone take that away from you!"

"As a first-generation college student, I was not sure what to expect. I graduated high school by the skin of my teeth and found collegiate pursuits more desirable than joining the workforce. Little did I know the most significant discovery of my undergraduate studies would not be interpersonal, but personal. I discovered a passion for understanding within waiting to be tapped. Now as a graduate student making preparations for doctoral applications, I've changed the course of my family's legacy and learned more about myself and my destiny than I ever anticipated."

BIBLIOGRAPHY

Books

Adler, Mortimer J. *Aristotle for Everybody: Difficult Thought Made Easy* (New York: Simon & Schuster, 1978).

_____ and Charles Van Doren. *How to Read a Book: The Classic Guide to Intelligent Reading*, revised edition. New York: Touchstone, 1940, 1967, 1972.

_____. *Truth in Religion: The Plurality of Religions and the Unity of Truth*. New York: Macmillan, 1990.

Aristotle. *Metaphysics*.

_____. *Nicomachean Ethics*.

Berger, Peter. *Facing Up to Modernity. Excursions in Society, Politics, and Religion*. New York: Basic Books, 1977.

Edward de Bono de. *Lateral Thinking: Step by Step*. New York: Harper & Row, 1970.

_____. *Six Thinking Hats*, revised and expanded. Mica Management Resources, Inc. 1999.

Bauerlein, Mark. *The Dumbest Generation: How the Digital Age Stupefies Young Americans and Jeopardizes Our Future (Or, Don't Trust Anyone Under 30)*. New York: Tarcher/Penguin, 2008.

Blackwell Companion to Natural Theology, edited by William L. Craig and J. P. Moreland. Malden, MA: Wiley-Blackwell, 2009.

The Cambridge Companion to Atheism, edited by Michael Martin. New York: Cambridge University Press, 2007.

A Companion to Epistemology (Blackwell Companions to Philosophy), edited by Jonathan Dancy and Ernest Sosa. Malden, MA, 1992, 1993.

A Companion to Pragmatism (Blackwell Companions to Philosophy), edited by John R. Shook and Joseph Margolis, *Blackwell Companions to Philosophy* (Malden, MA: 2004).

Germaine, Brée. *Camus and Sartre: Crisis and Commitment* (New York: Delacorte Press, 1972.

Carson, D. A., ed. *Telling the Truth*. Grand Rapids, MI: Zondervan, 2000.

Chall, Jeanne. *Stages of Reading Development*. New York: McGraw Hill, 1983.

Cooper, John, ed. *Plato: Complete Works*. Indianapolis, IN: Hackett Publishing, 1997.

Dewey, John. *Art as Experience*. New York: The Berkley Publishing Group, 1934, 2005.

_____. *How We Think*. Mineola, NY: Dover Publications, 1997.

Durant, Will. *The Story of Philosophy*. New York, 1926, 2961.

Dweck, Carol S. *Mindset: The New Psychology of Success*. New York: Ballantine Books, 2008.

Fogelin, Robert. *Understanding Arguments*, second edition. New York: Harcourt Brace Jovanovich, 1982.

Flew, Antony. *A Dictionary of Philosophy*. Revised second edition. New York: St. Martin's Press, 1979.

Gadamer, Hans-George. *Truth and Method*, translated and rev. Joel Weinsheimer and Donald G. Marshall, second edition. New York: Crossroad, 1991.

Geisler, Norman L. *Baker's Encyclopedia of Christian Apologetics*. Grand Rapids: Baker Academic, 1999.

_____. and Ronald M. Brooks. *Come, Let Us Reason: An Introduction to Logical Thinking*. Grand Rapids, MI: Baker, 1990.

_____. and Frank Turek. *I Don't Have Enough Faith to Be An Atheist*. Wheaton, IL: Crossway Publishers, 2004.

Gilson, Etienne. *God and Philosophy*. New Haven, CT: Yale University Press, 1941.

Goldman, Alvin. *Knowledge in a Social World*. New York: Oxford University Press, 1999.

Groothuis, Douglas. *Christian Apologetics: Comprehensive Case for the Christian Faith*. Grand Rapids, MI: IVP Academic, 2011.

_____. *On Jesus*. Belmont, CA: Wadsworth Publishing, 2003.

_____. *Truth Decay: Defending Christianity Against the Challenges for Postmodernism*. Downers Grove, IL: InterVarsity Press, 2000.

Habermas, Gary R. *Ancient Evidence for the Life of Jesus: Historical Records of His Death and Resurrection*. Nashville, TN: Thomas Nelson, 1984.

_____. Habermas, Gary R. *Dealing with Doubt*. Chicago: Moody Press, 1990.

_____. and Antony G. N. Flew, *Resurrected? An Atheist and Theist Dialogue*, edited by John F. Ankerberg. Lanham, MD: Rowman and Littlefield, 2005.

Halverson, William H. *A Concise Introduction to Philosophy*, third edition. New York: Random House, 1967, 1972, 1976.

Hendricks, Howard and William D. Hendricks. *Living By the Book: The Art and Science of Reading the Bible, new edition*. Chicago, IL: Moody Press, 2007.

Hirsch, Jr. E. D. *Validity in Interpretation*. New Haven, CT: Yale University Press, 1967.

James, William. *The Will to Believe*. New York: Dover, 1956.

Jones, W. T. *A History of Philosophy*, second edition, 5 volumes. Belmont, CA: Wadsworth, 1969-1997.

Kenny, Anthony, editor. *The Oxford History of Western Philosophy* (New York: Oxford University Press, 1994).

Kierkegaard, Søren. *Philosophical Fragments*, translated by Edna Hong and Peter Hong. Princeton, NJ: Princeton University Press, 1985.

Kohnert, K J. and Bates, E, "Balancing Bilinguals II: Lexical Comprehension and Cognitive Processing In Children Learning Spanish and English." *Journal of Speech, Language and Research* 45 (2002): 347-359.

Korb, A. *The Upward Spiral: Using Neuroscience to Reverse the Course of Depression, One Small Change at a Time*. Oakland, CA: New Harbinger Publications, 2015.

Kreeft, Peter. *Christianity for Modern Pagans: Pascal's Pensées*. San Francisco: Ignatius Press, 1993.

Kross, Ethan, Mark G. Berman, Walter Mischel, Edward E. Smith, and Tor D. Wager. "Social Rejection Shares Somatosensory Representations with Physical Pain." *Proceedings of the National Academy of Sciences of the United States of America*, 2011.

Lewis, C. S. *God in the Dock*. Grand Rapids, MI: Eerdmans, 1970.

_____. *Mere Christianity*. New York: Macmillan, 1952.

_____. *Surprised by Joy: The Shape of My Early Life*. New York: Harcourt, Brace, Jovanovoch, 1995.

Lightner, Robert P. *God of the Bible and other Gods*. Grand Rapids, MI: Kregel, 1998.

Louv, Richard. *Last Child in the Woods: Saving Our Children From Nature-Deficit Disorder*. Chapel Hill, NC: Algonquin Books of Chapel Hills, 2005, 2008.

Manson, M. *The Subtle Art of Not Giving a F*ck: A Counterintuitive Approach to Living a Good Life*. First edition. New York, NY: HarperOne, an imprint of HarperCollinsPublishers, 2016.

Martinich, A. P. *Philosophical Writing: An Introduction*: fourth edition. Malden, MA: John Wiley and Sons, 2016.

McDermott, John J. *The Culture of Experience: Philosophical Essays in the American Grain*. New York: New York University Press, 2005.

_____, ed. *The Philosophy of John Dewey*. Chicago, IL: The University of Chicago Press, 1973, 1981.

McGrath, Alister E. *Surprised by Meaning: Science, Faith, and How We Make Sense of Things*. Louisville, KY: Westminster John Knox Press, 2011.

McInerney, Peter K. *Introduction to Philosophy*. New York: HarperCollins Publishers, 1992.

McLuhan, Marshall. *Understanding Media: The Extensions of Man*. Cambridge, MA: MIT Press, 1994.

Moore, Brooke Noel and Kenneth Bruder. *Philosophy: The power of Ideas*, ninth edition. New York: McGraw-Hill, 2014.

Moreland, J. P. and William Lane Craig. *Philosophical Foundations for a Christian Worldview*. Downers Grove, IL: InterVarsity Press, 2003.

Moreland, J. P. *Love your God with All Your Mind*. Colorado Springs, CO: NavPress, 1997.

Naugle, David. *Worldview: The History of a Concept*. Grand Rapids, MI: Eerdmans, 2002.

O'Conner, Patricia T. *Woe Is I: The Grammarphobe's Guide to Better English in Plain English*, fourth edition. New York: Riverside Books, 2019.

Palahniuk, Chuck. *Fight Club*. New York: W. W. Norton & Company, 1996.

Pappas, Gregory Fernando. *John Dewey's Ethics: Democracy as Experience*. Bloomington, IN: Indiana University Press, 2008.

Pascal, Blaise. *Pensées*, edited and translated by Alban Krailsheimer. New York: Penguin, 1966.

Patterson, Eric and Timothy J. Demy, *Philosophers on War*. Newport, RI: Stone Tower Books, 2017.

Pearcey, Nancy. *Finding Truth: 5 Principles for Unmasking Atheism, Secularism, and Other God Substitutes*. Colorado Springs, CO: David C. Cook Publishing, 2015.

_____. *Saving Leonardo: A Call to Resist the Secular Assault on Mind, Moral, and Meaning.* Nashville, TN: B&H Publishing, 2010.

_____. *Total Truth: Liberating Christianity from Its Cultural Captivity.* Wheaton, IL: Crossway, 2004.

Postman, Neil. *Amusing Ourselves to Death: Public Discourse in the Age of Show Business,* 20th anniversary edition. New York: Penguin Press, 1985, 2005.

Prezas, R. F. and Jo, A. "Differentiating language difference and language disorder: Information for teachers working with English language learners in the schools. *Journal of Human Services: Training, Research, and Practice* 2 (2017), Article 2.

Rookmaaker, Hans. *The Complete Works of Hans Rookmaaker,* edited by Marleen Hengelaar-Rookmaaker, 5 volumes. Pinquant Publishing, 2002.

Salmon, Merrillee. *Introduction to Logic and Critical Thinking.* New York: Harcourt Brace, Jovanovich, 1984.

Schaeffer, Francis, A. *The God Who is There,* 30th anniversary edition. Downers Grove, IL: InterVarsity Press, 1998.

Scruton, Roger. *Beauty: A Very Short Introduction.* New York: Oxford University Press, 2009, 2011.

Shockley, Paul R. *Worship as Experience: An Inquiry into John Dewey's Aesthetics.* Nacogdoches, TX: Stephen F. Austin State University Press, 2018.

Sire, James. *The Universe Next Door: A Basic Worldview Catalog,* fifth edition. Downers Grove, IL: InterVarsity Press, 2009.

Sutherland, Jean-Anne and Kathryn Feltey, *Cinematic Sociology: Social Life in Film.* Thousand Oaks, CA: Pine Forge Press, 2010.

Warternberg, Thomas E. *Existentialism: A Beginner's Guide:* Oxford, UK: Oneworld, 2008.

Online Resources

Bialystok, Ellen. "Second-language acquisition and bilingualism at an early age and the impact on early cognitive development." Revised edition. *Encyclopedia on Early Childhood Development* [online], edited by R.E. Tremblay, R. G. Barr, and R. Peters. Montreal, Quebec: Centre of Excellence for Early Childhood Development (2008): 1-4 at http://www.childencyclopedia.com/documents/BialystokANGxp_rev.pdf. Retrieval date: 26 July 2018.

Child Welfare Information Gateway. "Child Welfare Information Gateway 2016. U.S. Department of Health and Human Services, Children's Bureau (2017) at *https://www.childwelfare.gov/pubs/factsheets/foster/*. Retrieval Date: 26 July 2018.

Hakkarainen, Pentti. "The Zone of Proximal Development in Play and Learning" (2018) at *https://www.researchgate.net/publication/265626894_The_zone_of_proximal_development_in_play_and_learning*. Retrieval date: 26 July 2018.

Other Online Resources

www.garyhabermas.com
https://www.iep.utm.edu
www.logicalfallacies.info
www.prshockley.org

Name Index

Kurtz, Paul

Lacan, Jacques

Lamar, Mirabeau

Leibniz, Gottfried Wilhelm

Lecrae

Leonardo de Vinci

Lewis, C. S.

Lightner, Robert P.

Locke, John

Louv, Richard

Lucas, George

Lyotard, Francois

Maimonides

MacIntyre, Alasdair

Malevich, Kasimir

Manson, Mark

Marcuse, Herbert

Margolis, Joseph

Marshall, Donald G.

Martin, Michael

Martinich, A. P.

McDermott, John J.

McGrath, Alister E.

McInerney, Peter K.

McKellen, Ian Sir

McLuhan, Marshall

Merton, Thomas

Mischel, Walter

Monroe, Marilyn

Moore, Brooke Noel

Moreland, J. P.

Muggeridge, Malcolm

Muir, John

Naugle, David

Nietzsche, Friedrich

O'Connor, Patricia

Palahniuk, Chuck

Pappas, Gregory Fernando

Parmenides

Pascal, Blaise

Patterson, Eric

Picasso, Pablo

Charles Peirce, Sanders

Pearcey, Nancy

Peters R.

Plantinga, Alvin

Plato

Postman, Neil

Prezas, Raul F.

Protagoras

Proust, Marcel

Reid, Thomas

Rembrandt

Rookmaaker, Hans

Rorty, Richard

Rowling, J. K.

Salmon, Merrillee

Sartre, Jean-Paul

Sayers, Dorothy L.

Santayana, George

Sartre, Jean-Paul

Schaeffer, Francis A.

Scofield, C. I.

Schopenhauer, Arthur

Schumann, Robert

Scruton, Roger

Shakur, Tupac

Sheldon, Sydney

Shockley, Paul R.

Shook, John R.

Sire, James

Smith, Edward E.

Socrates

Solzhenitsyn, Aleksandr

Sorley, W. E.

Sosa, Ernest

Spinoza, Baruch

Stump, Eleanor

Sutherland, Jean-Anne

Swindoll, Charles R.

Swinburne, Richard

Terkel, Studs

Thoreau, Henry David

Tolkien, J. R. R.

Tolstoy, Leo

Toynbee, Arnold J.

Turek, Frank

Tremblay, R. E.

Wager, Tor D.

Warternberg, Thomas E.

Watts, Alan

Weinsheimer, Joel

Wolterstorff, Nicholas

Zacharias, Ravi

Ziglar, Zig

ABOUT THE AUTHORS

Paul R. Shockley, Ph.D., who served in the United States Naval Reserves (1988-1996), is a Lecturer of Philosophy for Multidisciplinary Programs at Stephen F. Austin State University in Nacogdoches, Texas and full Professor of Philosophy, Theology, and Bible at the College of Biblical Studies-Houston. His philosophical areas of study include aesthetics, history of philosophy, moral philosophy, and philosophy of religion. His scholarship consists of a wide array of articles ranging from topics about aesthetics to beekeeping to Michel Foucault's view of war to ethical and worldview challenges in the field of speech-language therapy. Dr. Shockley is author of *Worship as Experience: An Inquiry into John Dewey's Aesthetics, The Community, and the Local Church* (SFA Press, 2018), and co-editor of *Evangelical America: Encyclopedia: Contemporary Religious American Culture* (ABC-CLIO, 2017). Dr. Shockley has not only given presentations at various conferences around the United States and numerous radio messages on forty stations, but he has also given lectures in Ghana, Indonesia, Israel, Liberia, Mexico, and Scotland. He frequently leads tours to explore the ancient cultural, geographical, historical, and religious sites of Israel and Jordan. His hobbies include beekeeping, gardening, painting, scuba diving, weightlifting, and traveling. His personal website is *www.prshockley.org.*

Raul F. Prezas, Ph.D., CCC-SLP, is an Associate Professor in the Department of Human Services at Stephen F. Austin State University in Texas. He has several years of clinical experience working as a Speech-Language Pathologist in the university, public school, and home health settings; primarily working with bilingual children and their families. Dr. Prezas has served as a bilingual speech-language evaluator in the school setting and has participated on early childhood assessment teams. Also, he has worked closely with school districts to provide recommendations regarding best practices for bilingual assessment. Dr. Prezas has taught courses in many areas, including phonological development and disorders with particular emphasis on bilingual and multicultural evaluation and treatment. In addition to publications in several journals, including the *American Journal of Speech-Language Pathology*, Dr. Prezas has written book chapters and articles related to bilingual phonological acquisition, bilingual/multilingual speech patterns, phonological treatment models/outcomes, multicultural issues, difference versus disorder, underrepresented populations, and school-based issues. He has been invited to present on bilingual assessment and intervention and related areas at numerous workshops, webinars, and conventions throughout the United States including Puerto Rico, Canada, and South America. His hobbies include songwriting, yardwork, the outdoors, traveling, exercising, and spending time with his family.

69517337R00122

Made in the USA
Columbia, SC
15 August 2019